Introductio

You are alone, sitting in the dark silence of your peaceful atmosphere. You have created a space of peace, tranquility, to nourish your spirit and soul. Candles flicker as you raise your hands in prayer position. You utter words under your breath, with intention, and might. The board game sits in front of you, or what claims to be a " board game ". You place your hands gently on the messege indicator. It moves as you ask your question and you panic. It is only a game, isn't it?

Chapter 1

The Ouija's Origin's and History

The Ouija Board or Spirit Board has been around for hundreds of years. It is one of the most commnon divination tools with the worst possible reputation you can imagine. People have made this tool out to be something evil, sinister, demonic, in which it is not in anyway shape or form. You can cut a carrot or your finger off with a knife. Your intentions are what you get. If you want bad intentions and these demons coming to your board sessions, then this is what you will get.

If you would much rather desire a knowledgeable board session? A lot fear what they do not understand and this tool is one of them. It is neither good nor evil. It is like that of a kitchen knife. Harmless or harmful. Through this book I aim to teach you what I have learned about the talking board since I was first introduced to it. In hopes that your sessions and view gets a little brighter.

In order to better understand this tool is to learn it's history. So we will cover the basics of how the Ouija Board became founded in the United States.

The Fox Sisters and their Mother spread the rapping of tables in the 1800's. They would hold seances, contact the other side, with many other participants at the table. Everything was dark, so the tricks could be done. Things like this did happen in the past. Serious users know this and avoid this. They became famous for Spiritism and are considered the founders of the modern day Spiritis movement.

Although their practices did not continue long, their ideals have been changed and better looked at with truth. Eventually they were caught. Soon after Elijah Bond had a board with letters and numbers. He used a small plank (Planchette), in order for the spirits to spell out their messages. A pen for automatic writing was done in this manner as well. Dating further back then Elijah Bond and the Ouija.

It was designed as a parlor game to be used nightly at parties and after church. It was common when I was growing up to go to church, and then go home, have cocktails and use the Ouija. The board was and still is famous for being used in cemeteries. It was thought of something as a game.

Story has it that Elijah Bond and Charles Kennard had a small tiff over the production of the board. From what I have gathered. They came together and patented the board together in 1891. The origina boards had no hole in the Planchette. It had three small pegs and a pointed tip so the spirits could point to the letters and numbers. Shortly after the board had a " message indicator " window. So we have these two wonderful men to thank for bringing this amazing tool to us. The board's home is Baltimore Maryland.

In most recent years the founder of the Talking Board Historical Society Rober Murch held a Ouija convention. Celebrating Ouija's 125th Birthday. So the Ouija is quite old. Yet new. The " Ouija Con " was superb. There was a fabulous plaque placed in a corner store, dedicated to Elijah Bond and the Ouija.

The board was also produced in Chicago. Haskelite is another Ouija " brand ". See Ouija is only a brand name. Like Prada or Gucci. The general umbrella term for it is " Talking Board or " Spirit Board ". I have heard conservative fundelmentalists argue over names. That however is not important to the situation.

The more people think badly and speak badly of it, the more people will fear it. You are filled with lies and self doubt. Never doubt yourself. Spirit speaks first you speak second is what I always say. Meaning your higher self is first not second. Second is your Ego talking. The one that says " this looks good ! ". All vanity is Ego. yet ego can be very positive for us.

Many use the board for negative intentions. Such as calling on mass murderers or " satan ". This tool is not what that is for. This is not advised and not what it was made for. The founders of the board never had these ill or sick and twisted view points.

There are also origins of the board dating back thousands of years, supposedly, into China. I have never seen the fruits of that theory. Numbers on circular boards, with dousing rods positioned in the center of the board, by post and glue. This is another form of the board. There are so many out there now. The Psychic Circle was popular when I was about 16.

I myself have had many different versions of the board. All down to the pink Ouija. The s maller boards are what I love. I have fallen in love with Miniature Ouija's. They are very handly. Direct Channeling is much clearer now for me. The board isn't always necessary.

There are Pendulum boards. You get a smaller square card with colors, numbers, letters sometimes. You may even get one that stands the pendulum by iteslf. There are that many types of Spirit Communication devices. It is a fascinating thing to dedicate your life to the study and work of Ouija communications. It is empowering if you go at it from this point of view. This is why I call it " Ouija Pop ". It is a small mixture of modern day pop culture into Ouija history. My own recipe.

I myself rather use a traditional Board. These just have a feeling about them. Some kind of vibe that makes you feel spiritual and empowered. My very first board was a regular old Parker Brother's board! Low and behold Santa did deliver that year. He came with a Ouija and a deck of Tarot Cards. That same deck I still have to this day. They are well over 30 years old. There is so much history and mystery surrounding the Ouija. Some find it quite taboo to talk about to this day. Seeing how far we have come with religious freedom you would think others might just catch on to the positive side of the board, rather than that of the flip side of the coin.

Many famous musicians, modern day celebrity's, even down to the man that came up with AA (Alcoholics Anonymous), use this tool. The entire concept of the twelve step program came from the board. Did you know this? The idea was originated from the use of the Ouija. Quite fascinating is it not?

The naming of the board has a quite interesting history to it as well. Bond, as history shows us, sat down and asked what it should be called. The board spelled out " O U I J A ". They had asked what this " O U I J A " meant and it spelled out " Luck ". While we know that O U I J A does not in fact mean luck it is from the french and german words O U I equals yes in french and J A supposedly means no in german. Later studies find that JA means yes as well. When attempting to find the meaning of the board oddly enough the woman in the room with Bond, had a locket on and engraved on this locket was the word " O U I J A ". So we can take this into account. I really do not think anyone knows just exactly where " O U I J A " came from, aside from the users that asked what to call it.

We can now see just what an impact this board has made upon society today. It has either left a " bad taste " in people's mouths or a good one! I am really striving for the latter. There was quite the " satanic panic " back in the 70's right when the good old movie " The Exorcist " came out. This movie, even though the board was only featured for 31 seconds, yes I have timed the clip, it gave the board a terrible reputation. This really upset the church when this film was released. Although I was not born yet I do hear stories of thoursands of people going home and burning their boards after seeing this movie. When I first saw this movie at the age of 5 I did not even acknowledge the board was in there. I didn't even in fact see this clip until recent years. That shows how little the board had to do with what went on leading to the little girl's possession.

So to wrap this chapter up we will go over a few things that the Ouija is not. First off it is not a tool of " satan ". Second it is not going to lead to possession. 99.9% of the time anything negative that does come from the board comes from the participant or participants. This is what we call a self fulfilling prophecy. One person has a bad experience with the board, yes it is their own fault weather they know it or not, and then it becomes evil. Or through word of mouth it has become very evil to some. If someone's friend's friend had a Grandmother that had a bad experience with the board then yes, it must indeed be evil. When this is the total oposite of what it is. Remember to always use common sense when using the board. It is not a " fortune telling " tool, it is a tool to delve into yourself and learn even more of your existance, the energies around us, and a very effective way to connect with our loved ones that have passed on.

Chapter 2

Preparing Yourself To Use The Ouija

Well we have come this far. Dispelling a few of the myths, taboos, and rumours that surround this " mysterious " Ouija Board. So let's see just how we can prepare ourselves and get ready to use it for our own highest good. You can use this tool to delve into your own life's situations, your own subconscious mind, you can speak with animals and I have even heard some speak with plants. I have yet to do this. So what all goes into a Ouija Session? Is it safe to use it alone? Will you get possessed?

To prepare yourself for a wonderful journey with the board always remember it is in the heart of the user that brings about what messages you will receive. Say you have a board and you want to pull it out and just start asking questions. Remember this is a spiritual tool and not just a game of sorry or battleship. So we must apporach this with respect, good intentions, and knowledge. Knowledge is key and that knowledge applied is power. So with what I am going to teach you I would like for you to take action with these words. Act on inspiration. If you are upset, angry, depressed, and you pull out your Ouija, you might not get the positive messages that you are looking for. Yet you just might get them! Our ancestors, Source, God/Goddess, whatever name you place on the Divine wants to help us. Source wants us to be happy, joyful, and live life to it's fullest. You are the one oporating the board here. You are the director.

When people ask me how to Ouija I always ask them one thing. What is your intention and what/who are you trying to connect with? This is so important in your works. You must set a very positive intention before you begin. This is why it would be best to plan a day ahead of time to do your board session. Cannot find someone to use the board with? Well, do you have trust issues that these people might not take it seriously? Go with your gut! Always trust that intution and inner voice. If you do not think you can trust those around you that you would LIKE to use the board with, then do not whatsoever. These people can and will bring negativity to your session. This in turn will probably ruin your respect and outlook on the board. Reverting us back to " The Ouija and it's Origin's ". The bad reputation it has. Fear of possession, fear of something coming " out " of the board, which this is not possible at all.

I also suggest that you read, read, read and did I mention read? Do your research. This is a must. Research the Ouija, speak with others that have had positive encounters and steer clear of those that only have negative things to say yet have never touched a board. Thanks to the world wide web we have access to so much positive information directly on the Ouija I am sure you will find these resources for yourself. They are like burried treasures. A pearl in a clam shell. When you do find these people it will be astonishing.

Many claim that it takes two to use the board. The directions even state this. Yet think back to the times when this " board game " was really popular. There was more than just talking to the spirits going on, more like a little hanky panky going on under the table. The reason for the male and female partners is that of duality. Male and female energy coming together to form that circut. The " loop " in which you want in order to connect with higher vibrations. This is not a must. You can in fact use the board on your own, very safely, and with great results. I am living proof of this. I have been using the board for around 20 plus years now and by myself. I just do not trust people to use it with me.

You also have someone to either; scribe for you, write down the messages, etc. If you can find someone that you trust perfect! That is even better. If not then do not worry one bit! Here is my " opening ceremony " before I do a Ouija Session. I always do these things and they will become second nature for you as well. You by yourself can channel this energy too. You do not need a partner. I don't anyway. I never have. So shall we begin? Are you ready to venture into this wonderful tool and unlock your hidden potential? Within this chapter I will be giving you step by step instructions on just how I use the Ouija. It does take practice and a lot of patience. Please do not expect to get results as soon as you pop the board out of the box. Expect the unexpected!

Planning The Session

When you are first starting out using this tool it is best and very wise to plan ahead. This way you have time to focus on just who you want to speak with, I would say stick with an Ancestor or aim for your Spirit Guides. Stick with one or two spiritual beings just for now. Just until you get comfortable with the board and the way you communicate. Each entity you speak with has a different signature. Just like that of your own. Each spirit has a very unique energy to them, a " tracer " or a " signature ". So what do we want? We want positive entities. This is why I say start with an Ancestor. So we have chosen our particular spirit/spirit guide/ or ancestor. Now get out a sheet of paper and a pen. A notebook dedicated to this practice would be ideal. If you are more high tech you can easily whip out your iPad or tablet and do this in your notes. For me I have been speaking with my Grandmother for over 10 years now through the board, and yes alone. This way if I ever need validation on anything that she does say via the board I can go to a family member and ask them about the accuracy of what she has said. This is a very good thing if you can get validation of who you are speaking to, through family members, or just by trusting your own intution.

On your sheet of paper I would say write down the date, time, moon phase, who you are contacting, your questions, and how you are feeling. Not only how you are feeling physically but emotionally and mentally as well. This is very important right here. The better you feel, the happier and more joy you radiate, this is what you are going to get through the board. It will be mirrored back to you. As the Universe is all mental then what we think about the most and radiate the most, must in return come back to us, according to the Laws of The Universe. Some refer to these as the Seven Hermetic Principles. Which are very good principles to incorporate into your Ouija practice. Find a time and a space where you feel comfortable with. For me personally I only use the board during the day. As it increases my dopamine and gets me pumped up. If I did this at say 9:00 PM I would be awake all night. This is one of the benefits of the Ouija, when you are using it correctly. Increased energy! Increased self esteem, increased health and some even say the Ouija keeps us looking " younger ".

Once you have found a space to do your work, you have your sheet of paper all filled out, you've gone over it for a few days prior to your session. Within the space you are going to create your atmosphere. This is the fun part! Get as creative as you want. Fill your area with beautiful candles, incense, items and photographs of whom you are contacting. You can place crystals and stones that resonate with you and that also bring in higher vibrations. A very good stone to use during spirit communications is Nummitte. Nummitte is roughly 2 billion years old. This is also reffered to as the " sorcerer's stone ", or the " Alchemist's Stone ". This stone is almost like the " xanax " of stones. It takes a while to get used to. You develop a relationship with this stone over time. This stone anchors you into the spiritual realms. Another great stone to use is Shungite! This stone is nearly 1 million years old. This stone, in it's pyramid form, connects the above and below. As above so below. It connects us and brings about manifestation. Having this stone around also helps ground you and reflects negative entities. It also protects you against harmful EMF's that our Wi-Fi routers, cell phone towers, etc.. give off. It is all up to you, the pilot, the user of the board. You are the one that is in control of this session. You are the one that is in control of what comes through, so remember to always be mindful. Selenite is also a very lovely stone to use and have nearby. Place this stone as high up as you can in your living area. This stone brings in the Angelic Energies. It is quite subtle so you might not feel it's energy at first. You will know it is working though.

Now I also reccomend that you shower before you use the board. It is like meeting up with an old friend you haven't spoken to in years. A clean area is also a big plus. If you can clean up, make it nice and tidey, then you go for it! This is only gonig to better your session. Not only making you feel better, knowing that you are clean, as well as your area, the spirits like clean as well. Remember the saying " Cleanliness is next to Godliness " ? This is what we are aiming for. You do not have to go out and spend a fortune on a " ouija house " or a small sectioned off corner of your home. If you have the funds and want to then by all means go ahead. If it makes YOU feel good. So now we are cleaned up, we've gone over our sheet of paper, we have our questions down, we know who we are going to be contacting. Next I will give you a small exercise that goes back to Ancient Egypt. This is called " The Heart-Breath " meditation. You may have seen this in many other books, yet no one owns this.

The Heart-Breath Meditation

Sit down and relax, let the days worries just dissapear. If it helps imagine a giant ball of orange energy coming up from the earth, through your feet, through every single part of your body, relaxing you fully. Do not fall asleep. This small exercise can be almost too relaxing. Let that ball of energy go all the way up to your head.

Shake your arms, legs, hands, if you feel this is going to help you to relax. You can even do a bit of Yoga before hand! What better way to go into a session. Once you are relaxed and ready to go on with the meditation do the relaxation meditation one last time. Now you are going to take one deep breath in, really breathe through your abdomon. On each in breathe you are taking in the energy of the heavens and the cosmos above you. See this energy coming into your heart-space, about the middle of your chest. See this energy mixing with that of your own love. Now on the next in breath you are going to take in the energy from the earth. See this energy coming up and mixing with that of the sky energy you just took it. Really feel the Alchemical reaction going on here. Now feed that with your love as well, just as you did with the sky in breath. Now on your next in breathe take in both; sky and earth, see it within your heart-space, blending and mixing, with that of your own love being poured into this space. Over time this simple method will become second nature to you. You will not even realize you are doing it. This meditation is going to raise your vibration. What I mean by raising your vibration is; you are going to be taking your own energy up a notch. You must meet your spirit guide/ancestor or whomever you are going to communicate with, with a higher vibration. We raise ours and they lower theirs in order to match ours. So it is a two way street doing this meditation before a Ouija Session.

Already having a daily spiritual routine is a very big help when it comes to the Ouija Board. Say you pray nightly, or you hold some type of spiritual belief system. This is all the better and will only aid you in your use of this tool. You may even develop a spiritual regimen after continued use of the board. This is all up to you. It has been scientifically proven that breathing through the abdomon relaxes us more, it increases blood flow in the body, it increases your over all sense of well-being. You can practice this meditation technique for weeks or months before you even begin to use the board. If it makes you feel good, if it makes you feel happy and joyful, then do it, within reason and within your means. There are many different methods of relaxation and meditation. True meditation is when we can clear our minds of all things, focus upward toward Source, and feel that total bliss. This is true meditation. Not a bunch of images and pictures running a'muck in your mind. Quiet the mind, relax the body, feel the bliss. This is meditation. You may find that you get sudden insights or feelings of just " knowing " things. I call these " downloads " or bursts of information. They often come very quickly and they go just as fast as they come. So make sure if you do experience this, write it down, record it with your iPad, tablet, or phone. These insights of " knowing " will really guide you along your path. You will also start to notice synchronicities. This is when we are thinking of that old friend who hasn't called in years, then the phone suddenly rings and it is them on the other end. Everything happens for a reason, nothing is by chance. These synchronicities let you know that you are on the right path and you are exactly where you need to be at that exact time. Almost like the feeling of Deja-Vu.

Creating Your Atmosphere

This is a very simple step within the Ouija process. If you do not have an area to dedicate your work to then a small space set aside, either outside, or inside, will work just as well. Creating your atmosphere consists of so many different, creative and wonderful things and ideas. Let Spirit guide you as you create your space. So what would go into your Ouija space? Whatever your heart desires. Just as you would collect things that resonate with you to connect you with that of an Ancestor's energy, this is the same procedure. I myself have the luxury of having my own space to Ouija. This I wish for all. Remember if you are still living under a parent or guardian's roof and they do not approve of this, you must obey their wishes, this is only proper and you are the bigger person in doing so. It pleases Source to see that you obey your parents or guardians' rules and regulations they have set for you. Afterall they only want the best for you. So if you are in a place that is not accepting of this practice please, listen to them.

You can very easily create a space that fits your needs. Weather it be outdoors, which is the best, or indoors. If you are doing this outdoors find a nice place that you will not be disturbed. Quite a few of my friends that grew up with me, their parents did not agree with Ouija at all. So I was the " one to stay away from " because I had the Ouija Board. I was raised very well by two amazing and loving parents. Now quite a few of these friends would create Ouija's on paper sacks! Yes you heard that right, they created their board designs on paper sacks. This is a very simple way to utilize the talking board. Simply take a paper sack, big enough for your alphabet and numbers, yes and no, and room enough for a message indicator such as a shot glass. It doesn't sound like it would work, does it? It actually works quite well and very just as good as having a brand name " Ouija " board. If you want you can use a bottle cap top! This can be your message indicator. Simply turn it on it's top so it the smooth side is facing down, and place a finger on it. Go ahead, try it and see what comes to be.

The main reason for all the tools, incense, candles, creating your atmosphere is to " anchor " you into that spiritual mode. You are shifting your conciousness into that of another. A more spiritual, cosmic one. Rather than that of a mundane one. In all my years of using the board I have utilized each of these techniques. Each one does work and they all work well and they all work the same. So weather you buy an; Angel Board, Spirit Board, Catholic Board, Halloween Board, you are using the same tool. This tool only happens to have a slightly altered name. So if someone tells you that an Angel Board is different from a Ouija Board they are 100% wrong. They are all the same. Just like a knock off Louis Vuitton bag. You THINK it may be real, so you FEEL what you would be feeling with the real deal. Get my drift here? I hope so. Do not be afraid to experiment in your own board making too. The more personalized the board in my opinion the better results. You created this board so what you put into is going to mirror back to you.

I hope you all know that when I say " mirror back " that I am in no way applying the " Wiccan " rule of " 3 ". That states " Whatever you send out comes back times three '. I do not believe in this whatsoever. This belief is something along the lines of " if you punch someone you will get punched three times as hard ", WRONG. Big time wrong right there. Although there is Karma, it just does not work this way. I am in no way saying if you are " Wiccan " do not follow your own faith's creed, by all means do so, it is your faith and your practice after all. Karma is a very tricky subject to talk and write about.

You will find Karma within Synchronicities. That old friend you havnen't heard from in years that we spoke of in the previous chapter, that is a little how Karma works. To me Karma is the basic beleif that if you do good, you will get good back. If you do bad you will suffer inside a great deal. All the misserable people that love to bring you down with them, you know those people in your life? The ones that when you are finished talking to them you feel so tired you could sleep for a week? That is their own negative Karma they are harboring inside of themselves. Always remember missery loves company. Do not invite that company into your life. It is not worth your own sanity. Trust me. You may also bring over Karmic Debt from past life's. Yes I am a believer in reincarnation. So I do belive that if we suffer from types of chronic illnesses, or anxiety, migraines, etc... this could very well be something that had happened in a past life and you now feel those consequences in your body. By the laws of the nature you must recieve balance from anything that you do. For every action there is an equal but oposite reaction. Many master minds have found ways around these laws of nature. Combating one law with that of another to get around certain things. In the end it all boils down to " What

Goes Around Comes Around " and surely it will always come back around. It might not be today, it may not be tomorrow, or the next five years, yet eventually it will come back around to it's owner. So be mindful of your thoughts and actions for they will come back to their owner. The owner being yourself. This is why it is so very important that you always keep a positive outlook on the Ouija. Know you are going to have amazing communications and get exactly what you NEED from the board. This will ensure not only a pre-programmed mind yet a safe session and many benefits to come from your communications.

Choosing a Board

This is the biggest question I get asked to this day. " Ryan! What type of board shoudl I get " ??. My answer is always the same. Whatever board that makes you feel comfortable. You choose what board you resonate with the most. I have been called to so many Ouija's over my life that I have had to sell quite a few to make room, yet I still have no room! Take your time in finding that perfect board because you know, it is going to be coming your way. By whatever means the universe decides to deliver the board to you, it will find it's way to you, and you to it. Is this not amazing? Source/God/Goddess loves us so much that " IT " (I will call it, IT, for now) cares about our every waking move. Yes, God/Goddess/Source loves you just the way you are. Do not change yourself in order to please another. You are being untrue to your being, and in my opinion when you change yourself to fit in, you are offending Source, your creator. When someone is making fun of another person because of say their skin color or hair color, they are making fun of, and spitting in the face of Source. This is not acceptable in my book. You do you and only you. You are here on this earth for a reason and that reason we may not even know yet but it is a pretty incredible reason. To be given this body and this life. The experiences we get to enjoy, the sunsets, sunrises, the love we share with families, friends, our pets. This is love from source. I love the quote, and I am not sure who said it, I actually think I told this to my Father one night. " Spell Dog Backwards ". So he did and he said " God ". I said yes! That is exactly right! The divine is in everything and our animal companions have unconditional love for us, as does Source.

So if you are unsure of what board you should get just browse for a while. There is no rush. There is no time frame in which Source works. So always expect the unexpected. Just before I really got back into using the board I was working in a local clothing store. A dear friend of mine had sent me a picture of a 1960's Ouija Board in an Antique mall. She asked " would you like this " ?. I said " Of course! Bring it to me ! ". Her resonpse was priceless " Good because the owner says she wants it out of here becaue odd things keep hapening ". I find it so hilarious when people get so worked up over a simple piece of compressed wood, masonite, or just regular cardboard. It is not the board that you need to be afraid of it is your own mind. It is the mind's of other's that you need to be careful of. So many can suck you into their own delussion of the board's bad reputation. After so many years of sleeping in a room with about 15 Ouija's and using these boards for 20 some years, I am living proof that most of what you here is just superstition. Yes exactly like walking under a latter or Friday the 13th! Which by the way is my Mother and I's luckiest day. It has always been our lucky day since I can remember.

When I was growing up we did not have the internet as it is today. We had email, chat rooms, and good old yahoo messenger! Oh, we had AOL as well and I still have my AOL account! So as modern day technology advances so do we. A lot of people do not like the fact that we are advancing so fast and rappidly, they decide to ignore it and tend to go back on their old ways of being and doing things.

Which is perfectly fine. If we were all the same I think this world would be pretty boring, don't you agree? I know of many people that are to this day keeping the original Ouija Board's design in tact. Which is a fabulous way of preserving history. We must learn from our past. So with all of this information I am very confident that my readers will find the board that they are looking for. It is out there for you waiting.

Chapter 3

How The Ouija Works

Everybody has their own theory on just how the board works. Each peron's theory is just that their own theory. So it is up to you to determine just how this tool works! Only put a twist on it... How does it work.... for you? In this chaper I will be giving you all of my experiences with the board, and just why I feel it works perfectly. For me this is. I will give you a few exercises so you can put yourself in a sort of ' reenactment " or " mock " Ouija Session. This gets you comfortable with the board. If you have fears and self doubt we will go over techniques to conquer these. Afterall you want the best session possible and the best information for you possible. First of all I will tell you that spirit needs all of our five senses in order to connect with us. They are so much higher in vibration than us, that all of our senses are needed in order for proper communication and connection. Now what do I mean by higher in vibration?

Have you ever been around someone that is so happy, bubbly, and always smiling? They are vibrating at a higher level than that of the everyday person. Spiritual people; Gurus, Monks, Priests, Priestesses, are all vibrating at a higher frequency. Think of it this way. In order to connect to the internet you must have a router, correct? Correct! The router is your " Ouija " the wires and the invisible wires are the vibrations. We must establish that connection and lift ourselves to a frequency that matches that of the spirit / Guide / God / Goddess we are wanting to speak with. When you vibrate at a higher level a very large amount of dopamine is released in the brain. This causes Alpha brain waves. In return you feel bliss, peace, you feel GOOD. This is what we must acomplish in order to make connections with higher beings. Such as; Angels, our Guides, Gods and Goddesses. So you are the operator. This is why it is so very important to " check in " with yourself on exactly how you are feeling on a day to day basis. If you are feeling depressed, sick, tired, you are vibrating at a lower level.

When one vibrates at a lower level, spiritually speaking, we are more prone to attracting the lower level astral beings to our board session. This isn't a bad thing yet the lower level astral beings often like to; play tricks on us, lie to us, gives us false hope, etc.. So we can see why it is so important to FEEL good when you are about to Ouija. Personally I take a supplement called " L-Theanine ". This supplement creates a sense of calm and well-being. It is able to do this by putting your brain in Alpha state. When you close your eyes and begin to meditate you go into Alpha state. The deeper you go the more likely you are to just fall asleep.

There have been many " scientific studies " done during Ouija sessions, on the participants, and not one scientist can figure out just exactly how the board works. They often come to the conclusion that it is all hocus pocus or the participants are moving the Planchette involuntarily, by the ideomotor effect. While the ideomotor effect does in fact have a big role in how the board works, this is not the sole reason that it works. We have all heard of the blindfold test as well. The participants are blind folded and then instructed to place their hands on the Planchette. The board is then usually turned upside down, on purpose, so the results do not come through. So in my opinion that theory is just that, a load of bogus. This is only limiting what Spirit will do via the board for us. They do need all of our five senses in order for this tool to work. That is just the way it is. You cannot get into a car and blindfold yourself, then expect the car to drive itself without getting into a car accident. Unless you have a self-driving car. See my point here?

A while back I wrote a blog called " Why The Ouija is Fabulous ", something along those lines, that I am going to share with you all. I am a very big blogger. I love blogging my thoughts and ideas, I love writing articles about items and products. It's what makes life fun and interesting. Like finding lost treasure. So without anymore of my mouth, here is my blog I channeled with the help of my Angel.

Why The Ouija Is Wonderful

How many times have you placed blame on an outside force that you've felt " made " you do something? Have you ever used " the devil " as an excuse for doing wrong? Have you ever blamed any type of Occult tool for the source of your illness or dis-eases in the body? For thousands of years man kind has used the old and outdated excuses, such as blaming the devil for your own actions, using a Ouija and then getting sick but yet it was the Ouija that made you sick right? No, wrong! It boggles my mind that people look to outside sources for a scapegoat, a way to feel less guilty or less feeble minded.

We have been conditioned as a whole, brain-washed if you will, to believe that if something goes wrong in your life, or your get an illness there's an outside source to blame for it. Why do so many have to look outside of themselves for answers when all the answers you need are right inside of you? Does it make people in general feel better to think that there IS in fact a possible " source " or scapegoat, to place the blame on? I personally think people can't and don't want to, or just plane don't want to try and take responsibility for their own actions. You are the creator of your own universe. You are the God or Goddess that source created. You are the reason for YOUR very own illness, dis-eases, " bad luck ", even down to the simplest of things such as stubbing your toe. People will always use a " demonic " force or some type of outside source to say " That made me ill " or " that demon made me stub my toe ". Is your mind and will strong enough to let go of those chains that want to make you place blame or scapegoat? Are you willing to give up friends due to the fact that they are so brain-washed into thinking " demons " and " devils " are the root of all things gone wrong? Or do you just smile, nod, and agree with them? All the while lieing to not only yourself and your friend (s) but adding to the problem as a whole.

From the age of 7 years old I first got my hands on VHS copy of Witchboard 1986! what a wonderful and amazing journey started from then on out! I had watched the movie as many times as I could. I had to have demolished three VHS tapes from watching the movie so much. At the age of 8 I had asked " Santa " for a Ouija Board. I knew he'd deliver and low and behold, come Christmas morning there it was! A William Fuld Mystifying Oracle sat under my Yule Tree. That day changed my life. Did it change for the better or for the worse? A lot will argue over my own personal works. A lot of people will tell you no matter what you believe it's STILL the Ouija or a " demon " that caused your Mom's X-Boyfriend's, X-Girlfriend's, Aunt once removed and her cat to do this and that, or it caused " terrible " things to happen! No matter how hard you try to tell someone your own beliefs and intentions they are always going to stick to their out-dated ways of thinking and belief systems.

Many people grow up around these sorts of things, myself being one of them. I personally have never had a " horrific " experience with the Ouija, demons, devils or any of the sorts. Yet I was not raised to think the Ouija or Witchcraft is " evil " . I wasn't raised to place blame on other's or " the devil ". I was raised and taught that we man up and take responsibility for our own actions. Weather they be good or bad, we do them, no supernatural force is influencing you to do otherwise. Why do you think you got punished as a CHILD ? Not one of your parents were going to say " I'm going to let you hurt people and encourage drugs on you, because in the end you'll get it from God ". That's psychotic thinking. It's not logical at all and makes no sense to me personally.

Sure I experienced very serious lashes from my own greed, during magickal working mind you. Daemon Summoning and the Lesser Key's of Solomon are very deep. Those I don't try to explain nor really use much. That's a totally different NOVEL, or even yet a Series. A very different subject in my practices. Things are very different when you are in a trial and error stage. Now as I am older, quite older actually which dates me a LITTLE... not much, few years, a year..

I do get sick and quite often. It's not that I live with constant dis-ease in my body everyday, aside from Fybromyalgria, I kinda say it's whom I live with that brings in these germs, viruses, etc... He is a Plumber and an Electrician/Contractor, a damn good business man too! I guess I'm just VERY prone to colds, flu's, etc... I do yoga daily, I eat healthy, a lot at that too. I live a busy life. I have a lot of clients and amazing friends. I've been using the Ouija for almost twenty - two years now and I feel like it's been such a help. It's given me insight into this world and guided me via my grandmother, upon her passing.

I do not and never will associate Spirit Communications with illness, dis-ease, hatred, negativity, ever... I think it's a really silly and childish idea or ideology. It's very Christian to me almost Catholic.

My Mother was raised Catholic so I can get advise from her on that topic.

I met many, many people via social media that are so special to me. People that radiate love and understanding, compassion and kindness. They've changed my life for the better and I'm humbled and honored to call them friends. This is what the Ouija has brought me. Love, knowledge, new opportunities, healing and hope. This is how I Live my life. I do this daily yes and still make no connection between the two topics spoken above. Ouija is an amazing tool and it's what you make of it. So if you think Evil is the cause of problems for yourself and others then that's what's coming right back at ya. I get a lot of love. I wish you all the best in Spirit Communications!

So you can see within this article I have writen, many people like to " scapegoat ". That is a basic unbrella term for placing the blame on " unseen forces " that are beyond your control. Maybe someone did have something awful happen to them during a Ouija Board session and they no longer wish to use this tool. It is all up to us to decipher weather or not this tool is for us or not. Simply by reading about this tool, using it, even handling one, you will know if this is for you or if it is not. If you are reading this book and you have decided that Ouija is your tool then more power to you and I stand by your choice! Once we get into the Ouija and the more Esoteric side of the board there are so many hiden treasures hidden in this world for you, waiting to be uncovered!

I am by far an expert in this area. however I do have experience. So what really makes the Ouija work? It is YOU. You and Source/Spirit/God/Goddess. When you raise your vibration to match that of your guides you are creating a literal Ethereal light. The Ethereal realm is a state of bliss, no form, only feelings. This is why you must feel good in order to have a good session. A while back I was mentioning the Ethereal realm, as well as " Ether " and how you feel that state of bliss within that state of meditation.

Once you create this light and begin communications, yes I will tell you, other beings will see this light and want to " jump " in. They like a moth to the flame will get a bit confused, if you will, and see this light coming from you, a human, something living. You give off love, you radiate it, therefore there will be times they try to pop in on your session.

I feel this is very much missunderstood. I feel that these beings only want one thing. What does a bully ever want? Attention. This is what they are seeking. If you feel comfortable and able to do so, you may tell them to " go into your Heaven ", it is time for them to move on and not bother you. This is all a bully really needs. Is some love and a push in the right direction, exspecially when dealing with a Spirit-Bully.

Spirit " Bullies " AKA: Negative Thought Forms

Spirit " Bullies " are we what encounter through the board, and often due to the light you are vibrating. They will find it warm, inviting, loving and want to get your attention. As above when I mentioned telling them to " go away " I really meant tell them to go away. If you have to get forceful then scream at them. This is what I do and I firmly believe that this works. You must WILL these things away that is if they stick around. It can almost be like stepping on gum. So people get this phenomenon confused with spirits taking a hold on an object. They do not possess the object they merely use it to gain your energy by manipulating that object.

There are so many forms of these negative beings being created by people. You have all heard of them, their names, which I will not mention. They do not deserve to be mentioned in books on the plus side of Ouija. If you ever do encounter these like I said tell them to go away. Get forceful. You are in control of the board, you let what comes through come through. You can make it go away. This comes from many years of meditation, contemplation and experience within the talking board.

Although it is very good to protect yourself from these critters I will give you some examples of these rites. The Lesser Banishing Ritual of The Pentagram is a very good ritual to use, in order to clear a space of any ill intentions. Ceremonial Magick gives us so much and so many rituals. I use about three rituals from a book called " Modern Magick ". It is such a good book, very in depth and deep. I do suggest that you take a peek online for this book. It is one amazing read and will not let you down. Most of the time when we feel we are under any type or form of " Psychic Attack " 99.9% of the time it is coming from our own fear. So it is very easy to get rid of negativity or fears in a manner that follows.

Pushing Your Fears Away Exercise

For this exercise I would like for you to visualize a blazing blue pentagram right in the center of your forehead, your third eye. Now before hand you will want to figure out exactly where this " Psychic Attack " is coming from. Close your eyes and in your minds eye " see " in which direction it is coming from. If you see a dark mist in the North then you would face the North. You are facing your " Psychic Attacker " or fears, you are standing up to them. Once you have found where the energy is coming from let that big blue pentagram appear on your forehead. Now take your hands and create the triangle of manifestation. Your thumbs should meet and form the base of the triangle just below or right at your eyebrows. See that pentagram getting even brighter and brighter.

Now will your left foot take one step forward and PUSH that pentagram away from you. This is a very simple method. This method has been used in many ways and in many forms. What you are doing is literally standing up to the " bully " or your fear, straight in it's face and you are pushing it away. You can follow up with a cleansing shower or a salt scrub!

There are so many tried and true methods for protecting yourself from astral nasties or negative entities. Always go with your intuition regarding any working you do, even down the the cleansing. If it doesn't feel right then do not do it. You want to do what is best for you. The more you use the board and build up a relationship with your spirit friend/Guide/God/Goddess or Ancestor you will eventually get to the point to where you will have a sort of " bouncer " of the board. Someone on the other side that keeps a close eye on you and when something negative does try to pop through, this " spirit friend " will literally bounce the entity off of the board. So you see there are many perks to gaining the help and trust of other entities / higher beings once you begin to really build your connection.

As I've used the board for so many years I have developed such an amazing relationship with my Grandmother she is now my " bouncer ". Any time a negative entity wants to pop in she will see it out. Ancestor veneration is very important in Ouija work as well. Honoring your Ancestors and those that have come before helps us to build a very firm platform to work on. In Egyptian mythology this is what we would call " Building on Ma'at ". Ma'at being the Goddess of the land and all foundations, she keeps our ancestors in the earth. Everything that is on this earth belongs to Ma'at. We built our houses on her, our churches, holy temples, etc. Pathworking with other Deities is a fantastic avenue for improving your sessions as well. You can and will learn so much from your sessions. Below is a small article I wrote quite a while back about the psychological side of the Ouija. This meaning; getting inside a living person's subconscious mind and planting positive seeds. So if you have a very toxic person in your life you can always send them " Ouija Healing " and it is very easy to do!

First you will need to meditate on the intent of contacting this person's subconscious mind. Know though that there is always free will. Yet planting a good seed is never a bad thing. Just be very careful when you do this type of work with the board. It may confuse you and cause havoc in your own mind. First look at yourself and see if you can find what is bothering you about that specific person, within yourself first. Can you find anything? If not then you can if you want, do the " Psychological Ouija Experiment ", and here is my story.

Psychological Ouija Experiment

Experimenting with the Ouija after many years (21 years to be exact) can be quite the astonishing thing! The results are unbelievable! Aside from speaking to another individual's subconscious mind while they're asleep is one thing, but to actually speak to said person's subconscious mind while they are awake is amazing and revolutionary! As many know me through spirit communications via the Ouija Board, Talking Board, Spirit Board, Witchboard, whatever you want to call it, another facet of the same thing, a tool of communications with the spirit realm atop sentient beings, plants, ethereal beings and so many other different consciousnesses to speak with. I've done this all before. It's been done, tried, true and trusted by my own self, validated by my own self, for my OWN self's spiritual progression and enlightenment. This was the icing on the cake! This communication was experimental in nature, nothing I've thought of before until this morning. It just dawned on me " it's time to contact the beast ". What in the hell was I thinking?

So for the ones that do see me on my Channel using the board and speaking of all things Occult and Spiritual, this was filmed and I am one damn happy gay man for doing so! If you watch you will see why! If not hey it's ok too! I'll explain it all right here. I set my intent very firmly. Before I even hit record I centered myself, took three deep breaths, hips to heart meditation, and instantly fell into that state of bliss, peace and the " current ". I like to think of the " current " as the state between being awake and right before you fall asleep. I find this is the best for me to contact and use the board, or any type of spirit communication or channeling.

The " current " felt amazing. So peaceful, blissful, simply pure love and kindness. My grandmother and I have codes before we get on camera. She indicated our codes and I was ready to see what would come of this experimental Ouija Session. I hit record and instantly went into yet the " current " again. Never really leaving the " current " just sort of getting deeper into it. I placed my hands on the Planchette and asked for " The Beast ". I asked to speak with " its " subconscious mind. I needed to know quite a few things. The list goes something like this; What is it that you (the beast) needs? Why are you so full of hatred? Why are you so filled with rage? Why do you take all your anger out on the ones you love? As I asked each question the Planchette glided in a slightly different way I've never felt before. Each spirit or being you speak with through the Ouija has a " signature ". You just know when said person has come through, you feel that energy! This was a very familiar energy. It was the energy of " The Beast " !

I continue my session asking " The Beast's " subconscious mind as many questions as possible, trying to get to the root of the problem, the root of " its " hatred and anger towards not just myself but the world. The beast had a lot to tell me, he had a lot to express and get out. I now can wrap my mind partically around " its " way of thinking. I could never condone or think like that but I do have a deeper understanding of it. This really was all an experiment, just to see if I could penetrate its mind enough to ask questions.

I headed to my altar, asking for Lucifer's Blessings upon my working and fixed my candle. I Place it atop of the beasts " honey jar ", I raise my energy, ask for assistance and blast that energy into the working, with focused will and intent. Having the " blood of the beast " in the honey jar itself, along with other essential things in relation to kindness, love and compassion.

My observations after this FULL day of magickal-workings is that; the beast is lonely, sad, depressed. I foretold this in a tarot reading 2 years ago, that I do have written down and saved. After years of work and commitment to my path and dedication i do see the results and reap rewards. Magick and Science go hand in hand...

So you can see in the above Ouija Session, a very experimental one at that, that you must be careful when dabbling in another's mind. Even though your intentions may be good things do and can go wrong. I will tell you a short story about a man I knew long ago. This all ties in I promise you this. This man was a devout religious man, followed his faith and his faith only. He had many children and a significant other, they are wonderful people, true to their core. The man was diagnosed with diabetes, the type I am not quite sure. He had fallen ill and had finally went to the doctor. Although he accepted the diagnosis he did not follow through with his physician's instructions, medications, or regimens.

He fell even more ill to the point of being bed ridden and then hospitalized, almost losing his own life. Why did he let this go and not take the proper treatments? He relied on faith and faith only. He truly believed that God would cure his sickness. While I admire the amount of faith this person has, which is huge you cannot deny that, don't you think? He risked his entire life over this. He then of course, for his family, went on the proper medications for his type of " dis-ease ". Do not let this come first. Always see your doctor before you make any assumptions about your own health. DO NOT follow herbal regimens and alternative medicines first and only. Always see your primary care doctor first. Your life is priceless.

So with all this being said, the board yes does work. It works because we want it to. We will it, we connect with the spiritual dimensions that are happening right beside us. Faith is a big part of anyone's practice. As you use your tool and get results you gain trust. Trust and faith are two different things. Trust is physical proof that something is going to make you know it's true. Faith is placing your trust before you have seen/sensed a Source of " all things ". Gods/Goddesses, all facests of the Divine's face.

Contagious magick is a bit like this as well. When someone is so spiritually, mentally, emotionally, and physically depleted and drained, this leaves the person's mind so vulnerable to the merging of one bad seed into that of his own mind. Hence leading to a type of " contagious magick ". I have seen first hand the dangerous and hellacious mental anguish one man can go through by being so weak in his ground. Man has to set up mental barriers to block these " bad seeds " from merging with his own thoughts, actions, and words. I'd like to think of it as a type of Psychic Shield that one can put up to push out the " devil's seedlings ".

For eight years I have seen " The Beast " be magickally manipulated by the " devil's seedlings ". The longer you are around one that is pissed off at everything and anything, hates the world, hates their neighbor, hates their CHILDREN, the more " seedlings " from " the devil " begin to merge with your very being. They merge with your own thoughts, confusing you, frustrating you, making you feel as if these are your own feelings, thoughts, and actions when in fact they are not. I'd like to think of this as " mental / mind control " through " contagious Magick ".

You walked in his foot steps, not your own, for all these years of purgatory. He planted the seeds of despair and the notion to give up on life it'self and your own family. Seeing as how strong " The Beast " can be I'm actually very surprised that " it " couldn't combat these contagious seedlings from that of another person. A co-worker in a sense, a friend not, a foe yes. You stewed in " the devil's seedlings " as he walked in front of you, thus " the beast " walking in the foot prints of the seedlings, were magickally " caught " by " the beast " itself. You " caught " these seedlings and they planted themselves in your mind, depleting it of any light it had. Killing your kindness, killing your body physically, emotionally, and spiritually. How could have " the beast " not seen this ? It's so very simple to see! By merely walking and partaking in " the devil's seedlings " you being so weak, ate them up like candy! How could you have not seen this ?

Everything that he did you in turn did to your own family. You destroyed yourself with this " seedling ". Eight damn years of these seedlings being collected, stored, and blossoming in your mind can now finally begin to uproot and never grow nor see the " sun " again. What do I mean by all of this ? When you are so weak in your own identity, your faith, your everything, you are so very easily influenced by just about ANYTHING that are stimuli to you on a daily basis. Now that we've seen how " Contagious Magick " works by the MOST SIMPLEST methods, we can now begin the process of Alchemy. Transforming that negativity back into what you once were, if there is anything left to salvage.

The process of transforming the negative into positive can be very challenging. It takes a lot of time and patience to get to the root of the problem, for " the beast " it has taken almost nine years to get to the root of the problem. All the magickal workings that were done on " the beast " did in fact help! They didn't take immediately, sadly, they took though and now I can definitely see the transformation occurring. So, from the physical stimuli we've covered, causing the root of the problem, the " seedlings " how do we transform all of that back?

It's taken me years and I mean years to figure out just one person. I feel as if I've had " the beast " under a sort of " constant observation " state. Always seeing what magicks would work and what would fail. Almost everything worked, that is to say in the Astral anyway. When you can astrally work on yourself and someone else for many years, you CAN transform all the " junk " into positive things. How though? How?

I will say one thing, one word, something that I've learned and that is DRAMA. You have to be dramatic within your ritual mindset. You HAVE to let the role of Pan or Dionysus totally empower your being. Take on that roll, live it, understand the Stories and History behind these things. Reenact it in anyway that makes you feel it's coming into the physical world. I look back at 20 years worth of Journals and Magickal workings and see I had not put much " OOMPH " into my dance.

Start within yourself and others as well. Get into yourself first, that's hard enough, or was for me LOL. Then transform your " demons " into Daemons. Go on and help others do the same after you've mastered yourself. It may take you a mere MONTH! Or it could take you quite a few years to master you craft and yourself firstly. It will come. It will happen. It's up to you.

We see now all the different connections between spirituality and our tools. We are getting very esoteric with this. These practices are mostly inner-shadow-self work. Meaning we go deep to fix and heal the problem. We have a lot of good evidence. Now to finish off this chapter I would like to share a story with you. A story where the Ouija MAY have prevented a situation from happening,

OR, just two younger teenagers letting their minds run rampid. All in all, I do hope you will learn from this experience. Sometimes it is BEST for us and our families to keep the Ouija " under wraps " at times. School is no place for the Ouija and I learned that the hard way. You may find this familiar if you have read my very first book " Musings of A Small Town Medium ".

Ouija Goes To Jr. High

This story that I am about to tell you actually hit the News Paper. If I remember correctly it also made the news. So soon after " The Witch " and I met I had another friend that had lived just down the street from me. We would have the best of times together. Halloween was our favorite Holiday. We'd go all out making costumes, doing spells together on Samhain, making masks, all sorts of arts and crafts. What a friend she was and still is today.

After I had discovered the infamous Ouija back on my 7th Christmas I had also found a new " game " board called " The Psychic Circle ". It was the most gorgeous thing I had ever set my eyes on. However it did piss me off quite badly. Having to fold the board in four ways to open it up, the round circular disk it came with would hardly move over the bumps/creases of the board. Many faults within that board. None the less we were dieing to try this new board out. So we did....

We got out the board and we meditated a little bit focusing on the spiritual realms. I had great results by myself with the Ouija but hadn't with the Psychic Circle so this is why I had a friend with me this time. We each placed a finger lightly on the disk and proceeded with the usual questions " is there anybody there ? ", "

Do you have any messages for us ? " and bam right after we had asked for a message it started to spell out something.

Oddly enough the board had spelled out " S-H-O-O-T-I-N-G ". We were in shock! We were so young and to think of a shooting was terrible. We began to ask when. It spelled out a certain amount of days before school was over. We both looked at eachother, in utter shock and disbelief, put the board up and never discussed it.

The next day I go to school and get off the bus. I walk up to the Jr. High School and there are police checking our bags! There are security guards everywhere guarding the entire school. The second I saw those officers checking back packs I knew it had leaked. Our messages had leaked some how, some way, by neither of us! Not one of us told a soul.

You can imagine what happend now. Now was the time I got labled " The Ouija Kid ". Which honestly didn't bother me in the least. I was proud of my communications. I was not proud, however, that our Psychic Circle session got leaked. This made me and my dear friend fruious! We both talked to one another and came to the agreement that it was not either of us. I kenw it was not her and she knew it was not me. Who would want to spread that kind of a rumour?

All in all I got expelled from Jr. High School. I was not allowed back on the grounds whatsoever due to " Witchcraft " and the Ouija's " Predictions " that did come to FAIL. Nothing came of those predictions, thank the gods! However that got out is beyond my comprehension. I learned one big lesson here. Never, ever , ever, let anybody in your school know of any type of " negative " predictions you get from any sort of divination tool. Who knows though? To this day I still wonder what IF we did not have the security we had? Would I still be here typing this? Would my friends, family, and teachers still be here to this day? I just thank the Gods that they are all safe, we are all safe.

This is why now is the best time to focus on the positive. Do not go into divination sessions with intentions of trying to " see into the future ". You just may get something that will get your ass in some hot water. So, learn from me and my mistakes, please, and never bring those types of messages or " predictions " to your schools, places of work, or anywhere for that matter. Keep yourself safe and if it is a must, keep your divination techniques under wraps if you have to. This is mainly focused on schools, school kids, and the younger amazing audiene I have.

Sometimes it is best for us to keep our practices underwraps. Who knows though in this day and age. Every single day more people are becoming aware of their surroundings. More people are opening up to the idea that Spirit Communications, Witchcraft,

Divination, and all forms of the Occult just might not be " that bad ". We have come a long way since my days in school and to all those that are in school I wish you only the best of times. The happiest of times and most importantly the SAFEST of times.

So we see here with this story that when you are with the wrong person, or people, you will get nothing but negative. This is the sole reason I have decided to go about my journey on my own, by myself. After this experience of using the board with a very un-trustworthy person, it has left me with the on-going fear of not to use the board with any body. For they will only bring in the negative. This is only me though and how I use the board and get my best results. I suggest that you really do your research and either establish the strength and solid foundation to use this tool on your own, or, find some one that you can truly trust which can be very hard to be. The choice is up to you in the end. Be cautious of whom you use the board with, for we do not know everyone's true intentions. Let this be a learning experience for you. Do not do what I have done in the past. This made the local News Paper and was blown out of porportion. If it weren't for that one person I may just feel comfortable, and trust people, to use the board with them.

Chapter 4

Adding Tools To The Your Ouija Session

Within this system of Divination you can add a variety of other tools to your on-going Ouija use. Yes you heard that right! Are you fond of tarot reading? Runes perhaps? Well you are in for a treat! During almost all of my sessions at the very end, I like to pull a few tarot cards, focusing on the session at hand. I will then lay down a few of the cards, I use the Cosmic Tarot, gifted to me by my sister. She had a dream that my Grandmother wanted me to use this particular deck inconjunction with the board. Low and behold! It has been over a year now and this practice/technique is going very well. So after a Ouija session you may be " iffy ". You may have a few more questions, or just want to get that validation. Try this out and see how you like it.

Tarot with Ouija

Right after you have completed a Ouija session for yourself, or for someone else. Pull out your deck of cards, do not put your board away just yet! Pull the cards out, using whichever ones you use, and whichever Arcana you like to use. I personally use the Major

Arcana from the Cosmic Tarot deck, for reason I have no idea. I just really " vibe " with the major arcana of this deck. If I am using the Rider Waite Tarot I will use the full deck.

Hold your cards in your hands and focus on the session / situation at hand. Shuffle your cards in your usual manor. Now I like to tap three times on the cards, sort of a " hello ", or a " I'm here " type of deal. The number three opens the doors. Now cut your deck into three piles and then pick them back up into one pile. Lay them out on your board. Do you see any cards that resonate or coincide with your reading you just had? yes?! That is amazing! You are getting validation and you are still in the " Loop " of channeling. You can keep pulling cards, as many as you wish, until you are satisifed. This technique is not for everyone, and it may even confuse you even more. So if you do not feel comfortable doing this then by all means do not do this. Simply stay with one tool, the Ouija, or your cards, whichever you prefer. We do not want you to become overwhelmed within your practices. This will throw you off balance and cause for future frustrations.

You can also incorporate bone throwing, runes, die casting, any form of divination that you feel would be suitable and fit in with your Ouija session. You are only getting that much more information and valdiation. Again it is best if you can go back to a person in your family (if you are speaking with an Ancestor). So make sure you write your sessions down and keep up with them. You will be so surprised to see what you've channeled when you look back at your transcriptions years from that date. The Goddess knows I am still in shock and awe over some of the sessions I have had.

Ouija Healing

Now this is one of my all time favorite things to do. Ouija healing! Ouija Healing, Ryan, really? What in thell do you mean? Well! While you are speaking to your chosen being, you can ask them nicely, to send healing energy to anyone you want! Yes that's right. Your " Spirit Friend " will send healing to anyone that you wish to send healing too. This is another amazing thing about the board. Sometimes these people will notice a difference in themselves, you may find you yourself feel better. Another amazing avenue down the " Ouija Hole " is what this is. There are so many things that you can do through the Ouija, healing being just the start. It really is an amazing tool to explore. Using this technique within the board is like a magnifying glass. It expands. The help of Spirit and Source helps things along much quicker.

Now exactly how would " Ouija Healing " work? Well, since there is no space and time within the spiritual realms, time being an illusion, what we send through the board becomes magnified, hence directing the energy needed, for that specific person to use. Our " Spirit Friends " often help in aiding this process. If you want to you may always ask for " Ouija Healing " even for yourself. Simply ask your chosen spirit / diety to send healing to a particular person, a particular part of the world, or to anything that you feel needs healing. Source knows this world is in need of a lot of healing these days. So it would not be a bad thing to end your sessions by sending out a little healing via the board.

Animal Communications

The best part of Ouija is that you can even talk to animals and your own pets through the board. In my experience with talking to animals via the board, they tend to be a bit " slower ". They have a VERY different energy then that of a human spirit or a guide. When I first started talking to my own dog through the board he would go very slow. It almost felt like small paw's on the top of my hands, and a tail twirling around the bottom of my feet. It really is quite amazing. Is your pet feeling ill? Do you want to know what is going on inside that little fur baby's head of yours? Grab your board! Animals are very attracted to all things spiritual. Mine had a change in attitude once I spoke to him via the board. He was closer to me, we gained a better connection, etc. I feel it really brings owner and pet even more closer. You really find out through this process just how precious your fur baby is to you. One of my sessions with my dog Chico, a very furocious Chihuahua, who has big man syndrome went a little like what follows.

Me: " Chico, baby boy, will you talk to daddy on the board, are you here " ?

Chico: " Tired..... Napping..... food... good food, wet food, sun bathe ".

Me: " Are you happy being here with us and what happened to Buffy (My old dog) whens he ran off?

Chico: " Her nose got her in trouble! I miss her and I did not want her to wonder off. I tried to tell her that she was going to get lost or hurt, she would not listen , Daddy, I am sorry ".

This is the type of messages that you may or may not get from your pet. I am very lucky to have this communication and my beloved Chico to this day. He is quite famous now aday's. He has no idea he is on the back cover of his Daddy's book either. Ever since this session, which was only once, or twice, we have been so much closer. So much more loving. It is almost as if I can look at him, send him my mental message and he will come up to me and rub me, as if he is letting me know he got that message indeed. And indeed he did get that message. If you ever get a chance bring your board around your animal. I hear cats are infamous for wanting to talk through the board and have the urge to " pounce " on the board as well. I find this to be the most adorable thing in this universe. They have so much to tell us and we have so much to learn from them.

So how would we go about contacting our pets that are still alive? The exact same way you would contact a deceased family member or a Spirit Guide. Simply tune your attention to your pet, focus on him/her, even using the board around the pet may increase communications. Do all of your normal procedures to prepare yourself for a session, and then connect with your pet. If you have come this far and you are having communications with your chosen diety or spirit guide then you can even ask them to send your pet healing if they need, or to bring them in stronger. It really is a blessing and a gift to be able to do this with the Ouija. I have even heard of people speaking to their plants. I have yet to try this one.

Now with the help of a dear friend of mine. I will call him " Mr. Mothman The Sacred Scribe of Ouija and Esoteric Teachings ", together him and I have done around a few hundred sessions together. This man works his ass off to transcribe my sessions and I could not be more grateful to have him in my life. He has been so good to me over so many years. I will share just a snip it of what he transcribes from my sessions. Let me tell you when his book comes out you must go out and get it. I mean right away. He has a gift and I am really certain he was a Sacred Scribe in a past life. Below is only a partial Ouija Transcription of a conversation with the God Thoth. Yes, you heard that right, the God Thoth of Ancient Egypt!

Partial Message From Thoth via The Ouija

Q: ganny are you still here with me? A: yes Q can you/we bring thoth through? A: aye my child Q: thoth lord,...hi A: hello my children Q: how are you thoth? A: immaculate Q: immaculate? A: yes Q: do you mind if i ask you some questions? A: no Q:in the emerald tablets you have said that you will rise again, can you give a little more info on that? A: have risen already Q: you have risen already? A: yes Q: are thoughs your birds out side my window? A: that is me, Q: that is me? A: ibis form Q that is you in ibis form. A yes Q so how have your risen there is a huge surge here in heka in anchent egyptain religion A my cycle has come again through the ages Q: your cycle has come again though the ages? A: yes, Q yes A aeons Q: aeons? A: yes Q: so what dose it mean when you revived, when egypet is revived and you have resine A: you are all being called to my priesthood Q: we are all being chosen for your preisthood? A: yes Q: so what dose that exacly mean now? why now? A: so much hatred in this sphere ' Q:so much hatred in this spere , the earth spere A: call me jesus or by any other name for we all are the same Q: call you jesus or any other name you are all the same? A:yes Q: by waht ever name we call you wether that be jesus or budda or horis or ra the are all the same? A: yes, all faiths are seeing a surge in people Q: all faithes are seeing a surge, like an influx in people floking to them A: yes Q: is that a bad thing? A: no Q: ok Q: so you have risen? A: yes Q: ok just wanted to clarify Q: so what is going on with egypt? i dont watch the news, which is one of your highly advanced tecnologys, tv, what is going on with egypt? A: egypt is under ruble Q: egypt is in ruble? A: yes, so much negative people and energy Q: there so much negative people and negative energy surrounding egypt?

Many people like to argue over wheather or not Thoth actually spoke English. The funny thing is that when you are a spirit and you are communicating via the talking board, yes indeed, you are going to get English! This is due to the fact of our own perception. How and what we perceive through the board when speaking with a Deity, the communication, will be in your language. It matters not if they never spoke a lick of English, French, or Spanish in their life time's. These are very high beings and since I do believe that Thoth is the same as Jesus/God then he must know English of course. Now I have gotten messages in Spanish and for one I am not very bi-lingual. I will tell you that right now. I know a few dirty words in Spanish but that's about it. Many will argue with you over this. Do not even bother or waste your head space with such none sense. Spirit knows no time or space, they speak in every language, throughout every culture and religion throughout our entire world, and what a big world this is.

Space and Time

Spirits do not know space nor do they know time. Yet they are all bound by the Laws of Nature they are in a very different form that we are. We as 3-D human beings see just that, 3-D objects. Some of us will see things in a more 4-D or even 5-D reality, which is really pushing your spiritual abilities. I often get this question " Ryan, I have to be in the cemetery, next to whom I'm going to contact! ". I will always tell you this, no you do not need to be in the cemetery to use the board, in order to connect with the one whom you are trying to contact. Spirits are not confined by space nor time like we are. Think of it like this. When you are dreaming and you wake up in your dream. You know you're dreaming, you are conscious, you can do anything you want, yet you feel no space, nor time whatsoever. This is how Spirit moves and interacts with us. It is almost like small " bubbles " that they traverse the universe in. So you only need to concentrate on that specific area or person or place, to connect with that space or that person.

Time is a mere illusion to us here on earth. Yet it seems and it is very real and we must obey the law of time. Even with billions of different dimensions that are vibrating right next to ours, and the Gods only know if that alternate universe/dimension has time or space. If it were not for time or space we would be in complete chaos as humans. Time is what keeps things separate. If there were no time nor space on earth all dimensions and universes would collide with each other. Crashing together, bleeding into one another. Now this would be a major mess, wouldn't you agree? So it is in fact a very good thing that we have limits, which would be time. This is the only thing that is separating us from them, the spirits, the spiritual worlds, the Gods and Goddesses's of old, is time.

To further your studies of time and space and to fully get a grasp on what all this means for us, I would say read " The Kabylion ". This is one small book with a powerful punch. Ever since I have read that book my life has changed. So if you can get your hands on this small gem by all means do so. Read it over and over. It will all eventually just " click " and you will be able to make sense of just how space / time continum works. I am no expert in the feild of quantumn mechanics or space. I do know a little bit but just enough to get me through my toughest of sessions with the board and to better understand the universe and how I can work in this universe.

All in all we need not to be in any specific place such as a cemetery to connect with the energy of that place. All things are happening now, past, present, and future. Parallel dimensions, alternative universes, all of these exist right here and right now. So there is no need to go to these lengthy rituals and rites, to contact a spirit that you would like. I do however have a story of two friends and myself actually going down to the cemetery, Salem Cemetery, no I do not live in Salem. This is just the name of the cemetery. The entire night was quite odd and something was very wrong and very off.

Ouija in Salem Cemetery

Way back when the internet was still dial up (I am giving my age here), I had two amazing friends, well I thought they were amazing, that's another story. We sat up in my current bedroom, carefully planning out our Ouija Session. I knew better, I knew not to do what I was about to do. So I do feel this is a self-fulfilling prophecy. I will go into that later. We all agreed to walk down to the cemetery and try to make contact with whatever it was that we were trying to contact. I am almost certain that it was one of the former residents that had lived in my current house.

The story behind my house real fast is as goes. My house was moved to this land, this land being tainted by a Murder / Suicide case. Mr. Apple had come in and shot Mrs. Apple and then went out into the garage and shot or hung himself. So this land is very tainted to this day. It takes a lot to keep things at bay. Going through the deed to this house every single relationship/and or marriage has ended in blood shed. Literal blood shed. Not a pretty picture I am painting here am I? No. Not at all. Now after all that had passed this house, the school house, was moved here and placed on the original foundation. Ok, so we have a house on tainted land, with the reminents of what was all forgotten all beneath the house. Mrs. Apple's ring she informs me , via the board, is still under the original foundation of the house. Which is now caved in with bricks and stones. Very fascinating things! Quite unsettling yet quite fascinating at the same time.

Now back to the present! So my two friends and I waited for about what seemed like an hour, for the connection to the internet. We had done a few searches for God only knows, what not to do, what to do, when entering a cemetery. We grab my board and we all walk down to the cemetery. We find what I feel was just a few rows off from where Mrs. Apple is actually buried. The summer night was beautiful. The critters that crawl around at night, hoot owls, all of the amazing animals of night and nature. We find our spot and we set down. We have quite a few tea-light candles surround us. Now this is a short story and I still cannot understand what had happened to this day. We all three placed our hands on the Planchette and what I now know to be Trance Channeling, we all experienced a " black out ". This " black out " lasted for about 5 minutes for all of us. It was almost as if we were all three connected at our heart level.

Personally I saw the inside of the earth. I saw the root systems, the pipes for water and sewage, I saw so many underground power lines, etc. We all came to and ran back to my house, which is not far. The other male in the group had a look in his eyes. You all know that " Look " of a drunken man? That was the look. He did not seem to be himself ever since that session. The three of us have never spoken since. That I am very grateful for. This is honestly my only partial " scary story " I have to share of the board.

Later on that night I decided to pop into a Yahoo chatroom. Remember all the Pagan chats we had back then? Well I had met one Witch whom I still speak to, to this day. She had informed me that we were all experiencing something very dark, by opening ourselves up to anything and everything. We were young and they did not take most of what I did seriously. So there are ramnifications of not taking a very serious tool, serious. This is why I also will not Ouija with any one but myself. I have many trust issues within this area. I like to consider when I use the board, that time is all " Me Time ". That is my " escape " or my " going to church ". It is so very relaxing and energizing, comforting and informative, transformative and educational. This is what should come of a Ouija Session. When you are finished using the board you should feel; refreshed, joyful, happy, and have that " Ah Ha! " feeling. If you feel; drained, sick, tired, lethargic, then we must up the vibration that you are at. This can be done simply by doing the heart-breath meditation. This will bring you right back to your center if you experience this type of session. One more tip before I sign off on this chapter, if you wish to cleanse your board after a session, simply take a rag, a clean one, and wipe the board clean. This is not only a physical act but a spiritual act of cleansing.

Now I want to share another blog I wrote quite a while ago. Many people think so badly of the board, yes? Yes! Yet these same people will use a; deck of tarot cards, a pendulum, and my all time NOT favorite, the spirit box. Are these tools all the same? Well, read the following to find out why they are.

Ouija, Pendulums, Dousing Rods, OH MY!

Why They are All The Same

Lately I have been noticing a lot of people wanting to " steer clear " of the Ouija board and turn to alternative Divination devices such as; Pendulums, Tarot, and Dousing rods. What is the difference? Are they all the same? Do they all do the same? Does a ghost box do the same as a Ouija?

Well! Yes they are all inviting spirit into your environment. Tarot, Pendulums, Dousing rods, direct channeling, is NO different than the board itself. It is only a tool. I love to see the expression from people when they realize that these things are all tools, and only that, and are in fact the same as using a Ouija.

Now with a Ghost Box you have no clue who is really coming through. These things honestly scare me more than anything. I would also like to think that they do not work that great due to the fact that they're only, quickly scanning every radio channel, picking up those signals, bits of words or sentences, and then relaying them back. I find this odd. I do NOT like the idea of a Ghost Box. If they even work.

Now for Pendulums and Tarot.... When you are focusing on contacting Spirit with these two tools you are doing the exact same thing as you would be if you were to be sitting with a Ouija on your lap. You focus your attention on the questions at hand and the pendulum swings to a yes or no, to colors, letters, and numbers. This sounds familiar?

So you see. The same energies and the same model is being used in regards to pendulums and tarot, as well as Ghost Boxes. The only difference is they are a different tool. A different tool all on the same vibration. That vibration is spirit communication.

When you think about a Ouija " releasing " " negative " spirits through the board itself, which is a complete LIE, then you MUST apply these same principles to other tools as well. This is why I firmly believe that a Ghost Box is far more " Dangerous " than any other tool.

We have NO clue what is coming through. You can't shut out the spirits, you can only turn the thing off. As for the Pendulum and tarot, yes you are connecting with Spirit and also inviting those (hopefully beneficial energies into your home) as well as your own energy field. You can also apply these same principles to "

Bibiliomancy " which is focusing on your question (opening up to spirit) to find the answers within a book.

So, are we seeing the pattern here? They are all mere tools. It is US that invites the energies weather they be beneficial or negative, into our lives and our own atmosphere. So the next time someone says they will never have a Ouija in their home.... they must by law, take away the pendulum, the tarot, and any other type of devise that works in such a manner.

By keeping your intentions focused on Source and the Greater Good, you too can be a receptacle for Source Energy and get the amazing and wonderful messages that most advanced Ouija Users get. No helpful spirit will TELL or demand things of you. They will suggest possible physical things you can do to achieve your desires, answers to your questions, and so on.

Be very careful in how you place blame on the Ouija. For all you know it was the " Pendulum " that " brought in that negative entity ". In reality it is US that bring forth the fruits of our applications. We bring them into this reality by focusing on them, raising our vibration, or lowering it, to match that of whatever we speak to, and receive guidance from. Don't scapegoat the board, don't blame it on the board, or another " evil " entity. You are the co-creator of your

So you see these tools are all the same. They all have the same concept, the same intentions, we just use different devices to connect with the same type of energies. I find it funny that Ghost Hunters will use a spirit box yet condemn the Ouija. You have no idea what is coming through that box, you have really no control, so how is this any safer? In my own opinion it is much more dangerous than that of the board. Make sure to do your research, study, and always keep your focus on the best of intentions.

Chapter 5

Cleansing Your Board, Safety Precautions,

and Why The Ouija is Not a Fortune Teller

There are so many ways to cleanse and clean just about anything these days, I am certain you will find your way of cleansing your board or if you start to collect, all of your boards. When I first get a new board, I do collect them, I will sage them. This is only a temporary fix. Although sage is amazing and works for getting rid of negative imprints it does not last for too long. Although, since nothing can really " Possess " a board then sage may be your best bet! So for a small cleansing ceremony you will need the following.

1 Sage Stick or your favorite incense

1 fire safe dish for your incense

your board

a little bit of earth (try to get some dry dirt / dust)

Now you can pick whenever and wherever you choose to do this small cleansing ritual. If working during the full moon suits you best then do this. If working under a new moon, when she is not visible, this is the time of clearing away and banishing unwanted things. So if we are going to use moon phases then yes, I would go with the New Moon or no moon. Make sure all of your items are safe inside their containers. Your incense and if you feel the need, a white candle for purity. Now simply take your left middle finger and dab it on your tongue. On the back of the board make three " X's " with your saliva. See them glowing with a brilliant, beautiful, blue astral energy. See these " X's " going into the board and clearing it. Making way for all the positive and the wonderful things that you are going to experience during your board sessions. You can use any chant or mantra you feel that is right for you. You do not have to say anything but a simple " I cleanse this board of all negative energy " . Now pass your board through the incense smoke seven times. As you pass your board through the incense smoke, on each passing say " As it is ", until you have reached your lucky number seven. Now lay your board down if you wish. Sprinkle just a tiny bit of earth onto your board. This is going to " ground " it and " anchor " it into this physical realm. This will also get rid of anything that may have come with it. Now I say it is VERY rare that an entity can attach itself to a board. Unless it was a personal favorite item in a person's life, and they had used this board. So if you can find out the origins of your board, that is perfect! If not that is just as good too. Now wipe the dirt off the board, wipe it clean, and bring your candle, board, and incense back inside with you. If you are doing this inside then leave your candle to burn by your board (in a fire safe dish).

This is really all there is too it. You have just cleansed your board. You are now ready to use it. How will you use it? Who are you going to contact? Remember all of what we have gone through in the previous chapters. Use your intuition, use common sense, and let Source guide you. There are many elaborate rituals out there for spirit communications, cleansings, and so on. This is the world of Ouija not Witchcraft or any other faith or path, or religion. This in itself is a tool for self discovery, knowledge, healing, and power. Always remember that beneficial spirits will NEVER tell you what to do. They will always suggest that you may want to say, examine your health, or maybe go and get a check up. This is what you should be getting from your guides or your chosen deity/Spirit/God/Goddess. If the spirit you are speaking with is telling your terrible things and demanding you do things, then this is a very deceptive spirit and I would reccomend telling it to " move away you are not wanted here ". Have your " bouncer " of your board, which would be your main guide you speak to via the Ouija, escort this entity off the board. If you are ever in a jam on the board with a negative entity, which can happen, we are not immune to this. Simply call in the the light of Source to burn this entity up, or if you are feeling up to the challenge, listen to it, talk to it, as a bully. Make sure you tell it to leave and there is a wonderful place just waiting for that particular entity. Most of the time you will be able to help " pass on " a spirit. This will become a regular thing when first starting out with the Ouija.

Ouija and Fortune Telling?

Many are drawn to the board due to the fact that they think the Ouija is going to give them predictions of the future. While in fact, it can give you glimpses into what may possibly happen, if you stay on the current path that you are on, it is not a Fortune-telling board. But why can't it tell the future? People ask me. The future is not set in stone this is why. Every action we take is forever changing what lies ahead of us. Spirit has spoken many times on this subject via the board, protesting the use of the board for fortelling the future. The spirits that we speak with often do not even have the power to foretell the future. Yep, you heard that one right. They are just like us! Only in their true spiritual form. They too make mistakes, miss-spell words, and give advice that does not happen. Now if you've had a session and you are told such and such will happen in the future, if it's positive this is all the better, if you stick on that current path you are on then it just may come to be. Below is an article that I had written not too long ago on just why this board is not for this purpose.

The Ouija and Predictions.

Why This is NOT a Fortune Telling " Game ".

Ok so here is an article I wrote a while back on the Ouija and predictions that come from the Ouija. 99.9% of the time any prediction from the Ouija can and will turn into a self-fulfilling prophecy. This is something we make happen, weather it be bad or good. All in all we cannot predict the future accurately because it is ever-changing, with our own free will. There are so many videos covering this topic as well.

I may sound a bit HARSH in this article, so do not take it personally. This was an article written towards the trolls we all had problems with via my channel. So here we go !

Alright listen up trolls! Not everybody agrees with or likes the Ouija, Spirit Board, whatever name you want to place on it. It is a tool that we USE not PLAY with. If you've never used one nor desire to learn the truth about the board then your arguments, rants, and ridiculous complaints are 100% INVALID. With that being said what about PREDICTIONS via the Ouija?

Well for one, guides, ancestors, angels, etc… DO NOT always KNOW what the future has in store for us! So these " Predictions " yes I put quotes around them, are ONLY that certain spirits point of view. They do NOT have all the answers even though they're in another realm. If things stay on the same course, then you have a PROBABLE cause for that specific " Prediction " to come true. NOBODY KNOWS except SOURCE. PERIOD.

Now to say that I am CONNING people is your own fucked up version of " thinking ". I wouldn't even call it thinking. More like diarrhea of the mouth attack. If these trolls have honestly watched all of my Grandmother's predictions they've actually all come to be! As the state of THAT current situation DID NOT CHANGE ! PERIOD. Do I think my Grandma is all knowing like Source is ? NO! Only Source, God/Goddess, whatever Label you put on your damn source of creation knows that answer! Then again we are only human so what do we REALLY know?

My Grandmother has done HUNDREDS of Ouija Sessions for HUNDREDS of people with a 98% accuracy rate. Things I could NEVER know, things she could NEVER know (or well, she did know !). So before you open your trap and spew none sense back your stuff up. Do NOT attack MY friend/base ! DO NOT EVER disrespect ANYONE on my channel. If the only thing you know is farming then how in the HELL is your " Opinion " even relevant to anything Ouija or Spirit Communications related? Answer: IT'S NOT.

Please don't waste your time being a keyboard warrior. Please don't waste your time writing to me if you have a mouth full of shit. Swallow your shit first and then think about the possibilities of life outside of " farming ". There is so much more out there than dried up dead crops, and your single minded opinion, hatred, and spewing of shit from the mouth. Again don't waste your time!

Ok that was pretty harsh. Again that was directed towards the trolls, so you guys can see where I am coming from. The board for me has personally gave me very accurate predictions from when I was about 10 years old. They were not very good predictions at all... The very first one that came to pass was my aunt's miscarriage. The board I had received from a dear from of mine gave them the lottery numbers only BACKWARDS lol.

So be very wise and cautious about asking for future events. Instead of asking " What will happen on this date ' ... try something like .. " what are some possible outcomes if I stay on my current path... " . Keep it very open and broad. For your own protection.

So you see although the board can give you insights into the future, the future is not set in stone. Everything is in constant change within our universe. I may sound a bit harsh in regards to this topic, within this article, the sole purpose of me being harsh with that article is to really get my point across. I do not want people to feel let down when they come to the board and expect miracles. Now I am going to let my Grandmother take over for a while and write. Yes she has helped me to write all four of my books this far. So I want to take you guys into trance channeling and the benefits of channeling. Here we go!

The Benefits of Channeling

-Channeled How To-

Stress while manifesting can occur and it does. It has for me most recently. I suggest a lot of grounding when going through tough periods, this I've learned through the years. Patience does pay off in the end. When you have a stress-free place, which is rare, you can create and manifest better.

Knowing my family is safe and ok is what I am referring to. This, at the end of the day, makes it all ok. I know my magick has begun. Having a good circle of friends also helps. Ones that do not down you for your practices. That is what Ouija Pop is all about.

Instructions on channeling

1. know the first voice after the question asked is Spirit.

2. You are tapping into the ALL.

3. You are not going to hell.

4. Pad and Paper.

Quiet your mind the best you can. I do this often at bed-time. Let all the thoughts go by. You will notice your mind getting slower, lower. This makes your vibration rise. You want to connect to higher frequencies. Atoms/ions are vibrations of energy, aroused, so you can program those like crystals, with your intentions. Do this once your mind is clear.

You can see your guides, or just see " energy " whatever form your mind chooses. Let that flow. Talk to it, write down your answers, you'll be surprised. Knowing you are connected to THE ALL or source energy, this helps too. See yourself plugged in, within your mind, to this giant, beautiful energy sphere. A mist of sorts. The mind is powerful. Mine forms Egyptian temples and structures.

Write and note everything you feel. Any smells, tastes, anything. Soon these will become like movies, for me they did. Interaction with them is necessary to keep the connection strong. You're tapping into an archetypal energy. Sometimes spirit comes through in the form of paintings, Ouija, tarot, any divination tool. I'm talking letting it go through you.

Using your senses to create something other worldly. A sort of transference of thoughts/worlds. Bringing those things back into the physical are doorways to the worlds themselves. Sigil Magick is one form of this. Concentrating on a sigil and letting it soak into your conscious mind. You take in this symbol and it becomes on with you.

This type of magick is used in everything from TV commercials. It makes you want that coca cola afterwards. You are conditioning your mind. In that sense focus towards positive things, and states of beings. Focus on the good, on source, the ALL.

Share what you write down or do. Show your creation. Let spirit be present in the physical. Transference of thoughts and works of art via spirit channeling, is one amazing thing. When you are doing it properly, your life improves, relationships, personal... friends come, and go. The possibilities become endless. Below is another article on some amazing synchronicities. While you continue your use with the board you will star to see these everywhere. Not just in your spiritual practices but within your mundane life. These are sign posts or " markers " letting you know that you are on the exact right path, at the exact right time, wherever you may be.

Simple Yet Astonishing Synchronicities

(My True Account)

So, the other day I had quite the day! I want to share with you all, two synchronistic events, that had happened in the same day. They were extremely profound when I actually acknowledged them, waking up from a dream-like state and jotting them down. Big note right here.... JOURNAL your EVERYTHING! It is SO worth it! I've noticed one important thing too. What you think about REALLY and I mean REALLY shapes your future. So that being said, never EVER go to bed angry, upset, etc.... Go to bed thinking of the endless possibilities that are coming! What will you create for YOUR tomorrow? I will type this out in the EXACT same manner, as it is in my Journal.

5/29/15

I had two strange occurrences today. The first, I was thinking what my family doctor would think of my spiritualist practices, if I were to tell her. I go in for my 6 month check-up, sit down, she asks " What's your faith?" Very nicely, noting that she didn't want to push beliefs on me. She told me to pray or " do what I do " to help/ in conjunction with my medications, to help with my mental stress. Very sweet of her! How could have she known that I was thinking this sort of idea, the night before? She is so cute pregnant, btw!

Second, I was mowing the lawn, a very mundane task, yes? My grandparents show up ALL around me while I was mowing. They gave me guidance, love and encouragement, to keep going. (These were the two days I had not used the Ouija to communicate with them, I did feel bad). Reminding me of how both/all worlds/realms co-exist. It felt like the spiritual worlds were bleeding into this reality. Crazy what synchronicities come!   I have my guides/spirits REGARDLESS of the Ouija.

So, yes, all that does seem very VERY mundane! When you take a minute to look back at what you've actually thought about the day PRIOR to something happening like this, seeing it in your journal, going back and reminiscing your thoughts, it's incredible! You HONESTLY do create your own reality. The possibilities now, truly ARE endless! Now for an extra added bonus even more on Ouija healing!

Manifesting Your Daily Events.

(Ouija Healing)

Last night my Father and I had a very long conversation. We walked about the acre of land we own, looking at the pines, the oaks, apple blossoms and lilac trees. Both of us barefoot, earthing ourselves without him even knowing he's connecting himself with the Earth's energy. We had a nice chatter about loved ones, family, work, etc. We walk around one of our giant white pine tree's and a HUGE grey-sponge-mushroom was right there, in plane sight. So, he tells me to wait until today, to go out and pick it.

I wake up today, very excited about our small " walk-about " from last night. I pick the mushroom, which had grown even more, since they only grow for 16-18 hours after they've sprouted. He comes home from work today, early, not feeling too well. I said ok, hold on just a second, would you at least humor me, I'd love to show you something through the Ouija. He just kinda shook his head and agreed, he'd watch as I contacted my Grandma. He told me he started feeling better, like his lungs were expanding and filling with air.

My grandma had already come through, without him even knowing. The entire time he's saying " you know it's just the ideomotor effect ", I brushed that off quickly. He's giving me the benefit of the doubt here, so I ask one of his FAVORITE questions, " Ganny, where can my Father, find a TON of mushrooms, grey's to be precise?" She spelled out the exact location, street sign, the name of the woods, the land marks, all of it. Now he knows I have NO IDEA where this place is. He's looking a bit puzzled now.

I say " ok, Ganny, what can we do to help increase his chances, give him a bit of luck ? " I was wishing she'd say something like " you don't need luck ", nope! She went on to say

" Take one Hematite Stone, hold it in your hand, your left hand, see those mushrooms, feel them, feel the dirt on the ground, separating the mushroom from the Earth. Let that energy flow into the stone, the stone is programed, now go find your MONEY. "

We were both very confused about what she meant by " now go find your money ". Mushrooms around here, everywhere I do believe are very HIGHLY PRICED. I gave my Father the stone, he did as she instructed. His little brother just pulled in, so I hurried up and thanked her, the session was over.

While he's out hunting for mushrooms, I did my normal thing, daily house hold things, the oh so much fun, things... lol... He calls me! I answer and he says meet me outside in 10 minutes, I'm on my way home and I've got goodies. I almost slam the phone down, not doubting he found EXACTLY what my grandmother described.

Note My Father and Grandmother were VERY close his entire life.

I'm outside and he pulls up with his little brother, both smiling from ear to ear, we ALL have that smile when we have food ;) He jumps out and shows me the bag of mushrooms. Grey Sponges, like she had said. He then pulls his wallet out, $40 dollars he found on the ground, of this woods.

The directions were very accurate and detailed via the Board. He offered me $20, I refused. I felt like I was being paid for something Spirit inspired. A lot would like to call all of this " bogus " , " Stupid " or " Coincidence ". Synchronicity is what it is. Being connected to Spirit, ourselves, loved ones and guides. Even if you connect with your pets.

Now tell me how i'm going to open the gates of hell through the Ouija Board, after using it for 20 years. ;)

Yes that was VERY inspired by a fabulous woman. She is a Ouijaologist ! Karen A. Dahlman, so if you want to know even MORE ... look her up! Not all of us bite. ;)

It's not often you come across, I guess you would call this a " Journal Entry ", Blog.. etc. Of POSITIVE Ouija Stories. Why not start? What has changed for the better, through this tool? Not even Ouija.... Tarot, Bone Reading, runes. This not only brought a Father and Son together MORE... it healed.

Isn't Ouija healing and manifesting your day to day reality amazing? This too you can do! It is very simple. You are the co-creator of your universe. You are Source! You have that divine spark within you, that Source gave you, to use.

Now when you go to a search engine and type in " Ouija " so many terrible things pop up. So many misconceptions about the board, horror stories, you name it, anything bad people will use the board as a scape goat or play the blame game with this tool. You will find it everywhere! So here are five true stories, all very positive about the Ouija. You don't see many of these flying around the internet now do ya? People only want to hear the horror stories and feel the thrill of being scared. Well it is time to push all that away and see the board for what it is. One incredible tool

My 5 True Stories Of Peace Love and Healing

Through

The Ouija Board

1.

About 4 years ago I was using my Ouija one night, outside by the bonfire. I had no particular set of questions, just ONE intent. That intent was of pure love, nothing less. I relaxed and got into my " groove " if you will, placed my hands on the Planchette and let it glide around the board. The people with me weren't very much into this sort of thing. I asked my grandfather's girlfriend who " Anita " was. She looked at me in complete shock. " how could you know this ? ! " She gulped. I looked at her and asked her if her daughter visited her in her dreams. She looked at me with tears in her eyes. Her daughter did pass quite a few years prior to this. The message " Anita " gave me was

" Mom, Love you, Do not worry, I am safe, I am happy, I am loved, I am warm. "

She got up out of her seat, tears rolling down her face, looked me straight in the eyes and said " Thank you so much, I now have validation that she is safe and visiting me in my dreams, I don't know how to even tell you how grateful I am for you". I hugged her so tightly as she did me.

2.

Right after my grandmother had passed away, Veronica, you all know her, I'm SURE! :) I was devastated. Being the typical 22 year old I turned DIRECTLY to my pain pills. Popping at least 10 Vicodin a day, AT LEAST. I had woken up in the middle of the night, for no reason but the urge to use the Ouija. So, I started a pot of coffee. Just to kind of wake myself up and get rid of the nasty Vicodin " buzz ". I sat down and said as loudly as I could " Ganny! Please, from the bottom of my heart, I ask you to come here and be with me, show me you're ok, show me you're not in " hell ". She did commit suicide. I was told at HER funeral, she was burning in hell, from the Pastor. Let's just say I'm not allowed to be around this man now.

I'm sitting there balling my eyes out, still realizing what had happened. I barely even have my hand on the Planchette and it starts to rapidly move. I'm thinking this has got to be me, I've taken too many pain pills. The very FIRST words she spelled out were

" Rye Whiskey, Rye Whiskey, Rye Whiskey I cry, If I don't get my whiskey I surely will die "

At this point I KNEW with every fiber of my being, that his was her. She had made contact, just as she told me she would. We talked for what seemed like 5 minutes, which ended up becoming 5 AM.

I would never EVER recommend ANYONE using the Ouija under the influence! Just a little side note there. This was my validation, my closure! Everything we had talked about before she took her life, she told me, via the Ouija. I didn't abuse Pain Killers ever since. I got my healing, my " Ganny " back! Who needs those pills when you have your grandmother coming to you on this " cosmic phone ".

3.

This story took place about 2 or 3 weeks ago. I got a message about doing Question and Answers, Via the Ouija, as I do on my channel. Of course I will, I'm always open to suggestions! All the questions had been answered, I'm finishing up my session, closing the " door ". I start to see images in my head, I close my eyes and instantly I see these women! Out of no where, these women are coming to me. I'm thinking ok, what the hell is going on. I'll call the woman with the question " Tiffany ".

Tiffany had wanted me to contact her grandmother to see who had been watching over her daughter. All the answers were correct and accurate. The best part though, was after the Ouija session had ended. I accidentally started to channel Tiffany's Great Grandmother and Grandmother. I had no idea what these women looked like, just what I had in my minds eye. Tiffany sent me a picture of these two women and man, I saw. She is SO grateful and still to this day, thanks me for the comfort and healing she had received from this.

4.

I decided it was finally time to try and contact my basset hound that had ran off, when I brought my Chihuahua back home with me. I set my intent to contact her, did my meditation with my rose quartz as I usually do. I got into my comfort zone, calm, relaxed and peaceful. I placed the picture of my beloved Buffy beside the board.

Placing my hands on the Planchette very gently I called out to her. " Buff..... Buffy, Baby girl... My sweet baby girl, come talk to Daddy, please baby girl... "

The Planchette started to move in a way I had never felt. It almost felt like small paw's on my own hands, guiding them. Lo and behold, it was Buffy! Prior, we had no idea what had happened to her. All we knew is that she ran off, in the fog, with my Chihuahua Chico. Animals lovers, you all know what it's like when you loose an animal. It's like loosing a family member, they ARE a part of your family. Her movement was very slow, very " all over the place ", if you will.

Her words were so different than that of a human. She said very few words to me.

" Dad.... Road....Highway....Cold.... Love you....Love my house... No small dog. Safe now, warm, happy, love u "

Now anybody that's subscribed to my YouTube Channel has seen this video. You don't see the behind the scenes. I was in tears when the camera stopped. I knew with all my heart, it was my baby girl! My Buffy, she finally came through, after all these years! From this session I gained the most healing of all. Finally knowing what had happened to her, why she had ran off and left us. It's still very sad to think of, of course! I know now though that she is with me all the time, she's warm, happy and in a fabulous place.

5.

I think this story is the most healing I've ever received from the Ouija. There was and still is, so much controversy surrounding my Ganny's suicide. Was it something someone planted in her head? She was very ill after all, sick, couldn't move, could hardly get out of bed. She couldn't even open a pack of cigarettes by herself, this showed how weak she was. How sick she was, it was a terrible thing to watch.

I'm not going to go into detail about what was actually said through the Board, I will say this however..... I now know, from my Grandmother EVERY SINGLE detail, down to the exact time she shot herself. Now that doesn't sound very healing does it? No, it doesn't! It is the most comforting thing to know though. I can finally be at PEACE and know she is in her perfect " image ", that she wants to be seen in. Just knowing the details surrounding what had happened, did in fact heal me, my mother, father and quite a few other family members. Everybody is pretty skeptical about the Ouija, so they're still not 100% sure, it still brings them comfort to know that she is ok.

Talking to her on a daily basis, even without the Board, is the best thing in this world. Feeling her gentle touch, the smell of her lotions, creams and perfumes. It's just a phenomenal thing! Seeing her face as she was before she got so sick, is healing in itself. If it weren't for the use of this tool, I honestly do not think I'd be here today, typing this for you all to read.

In conclusion, I thank you all humbly. I thank you for listening to my Sessions, Watching the videos, asking me to contact your own loved ones. The peace, the thank you's, the pure gratitude that comes from you all, is healing for me as well. We are all connected, we are all one. If you heal, I heal. When you're happy I'm happy. We heal, learn and grow SO much through the use of these divination tools. I want to thank Karen A. Dahlman, Robert Murch, A.g. Ruff, Janet, Rob, " Tiffany " and EVERYONE that I've become close with, made friends with, all through........ The Ouija Board.

Now to end this chapter with a Ouija session from a very dear friend I will call " Elm Ouija ". Her encounters with the board are what I have spoke of in previous chapters. This is what you are looking to get from a helpful spirit. Good advice and care. The highest beings always have our best intentions in mind and her guide most certainly did.

True OUIJA Story of Empowerment and Encouragement

' There must be a Demon telling me to clean my life up and stop taking in chemicals, that are killing us, cuz that's what a demon wants to waste it's time on...." ~ Ryan.

"5/16/2015 Ouija

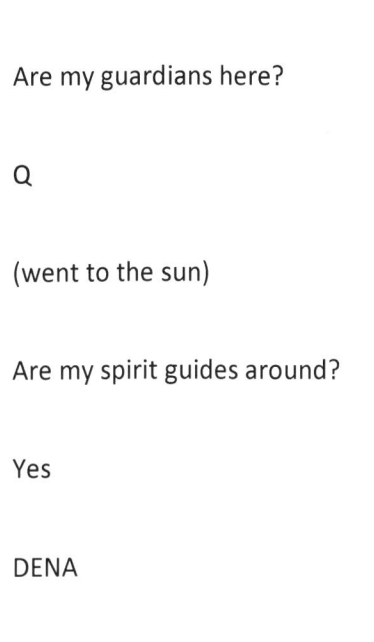

Are my guardians here?

Q

(went to the sun)

Are my spirit guides around?

Yes

DENA

Edena, is that your name?

YES

Went to the sun, what does that mean?

GGOD IS GOOD

YES

God is good

I've been called to the board, can you tell me any messages?

B QUIT SMOKING

KILLING YOU

Killing you, is that what you're saying?

BAE (?)

Babe, (?) is that what you are trying to say?

EAT HEALTHY

Went to the sun?

YES

LAZY

YES

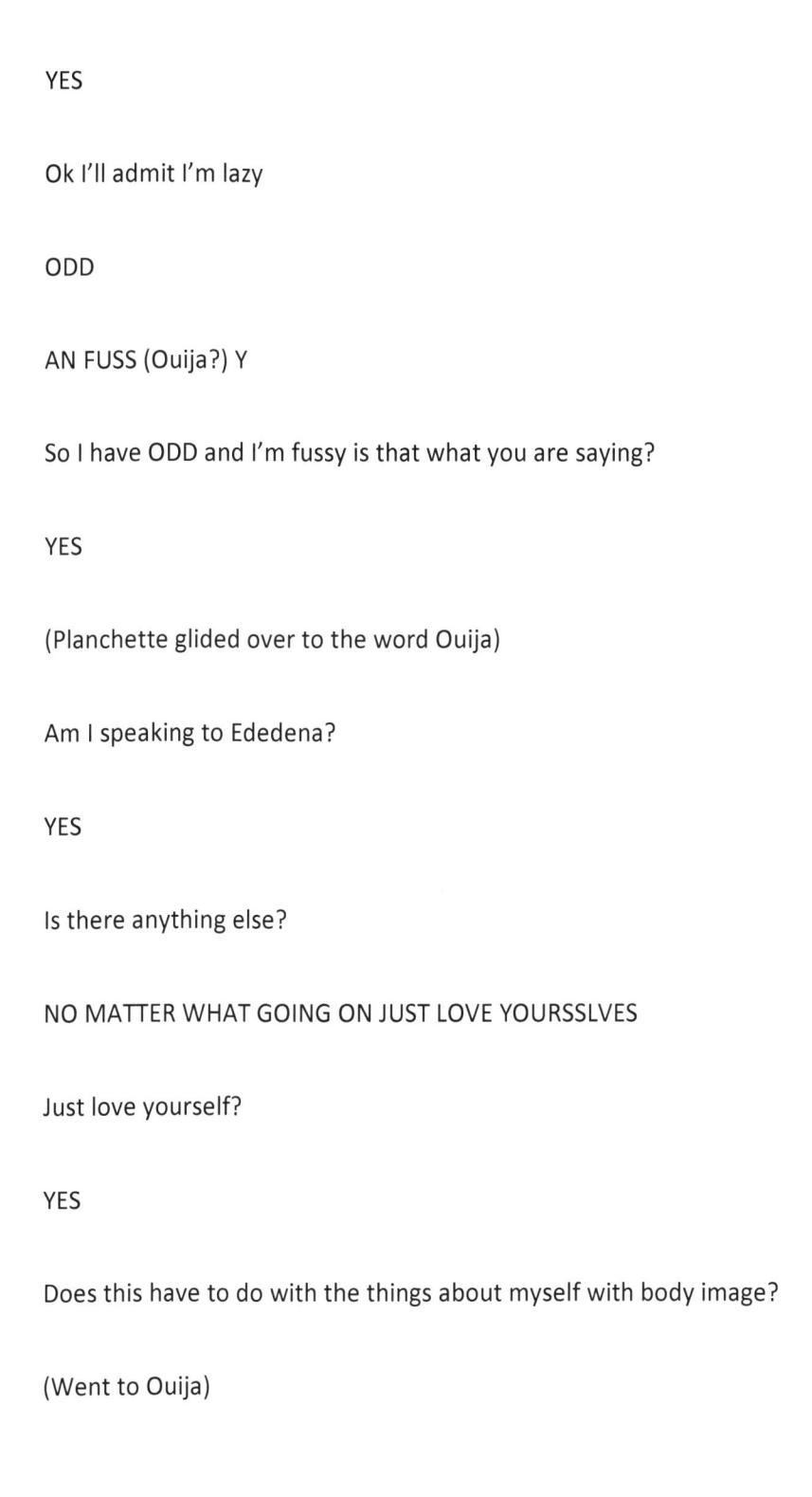

Ok I'll admit I'm lazy

ODD

AN FUSS (Ouija?) Y

So I have ODD and I'm fussy is that what you are saying?

YES

(Planchette glided over to the word Ouija)

Am I speaking to Ededena?

YES

Is there anything else?

NO MATTER WHAT GOING ON JUST LOVE YOURSSLVES

Just love yourself?

YES

Does this have to do with the things about myself with body image?

(Went to Ouija)

YES

What about the Ouija? Messages for me on that?

OUIJA IS A GOOD PUBLIC TOOL

Ouija is a good public tool?

YES

May I ask a question about you Ededena?

YES

(Ouija again)

Are you male or female?

MALE

Have you been on this planet before? Have you lived a life on this planet before?

(Going in circles, trying to get energy?)

YES

Can you tell me what time or year you lived here?

191(7)?

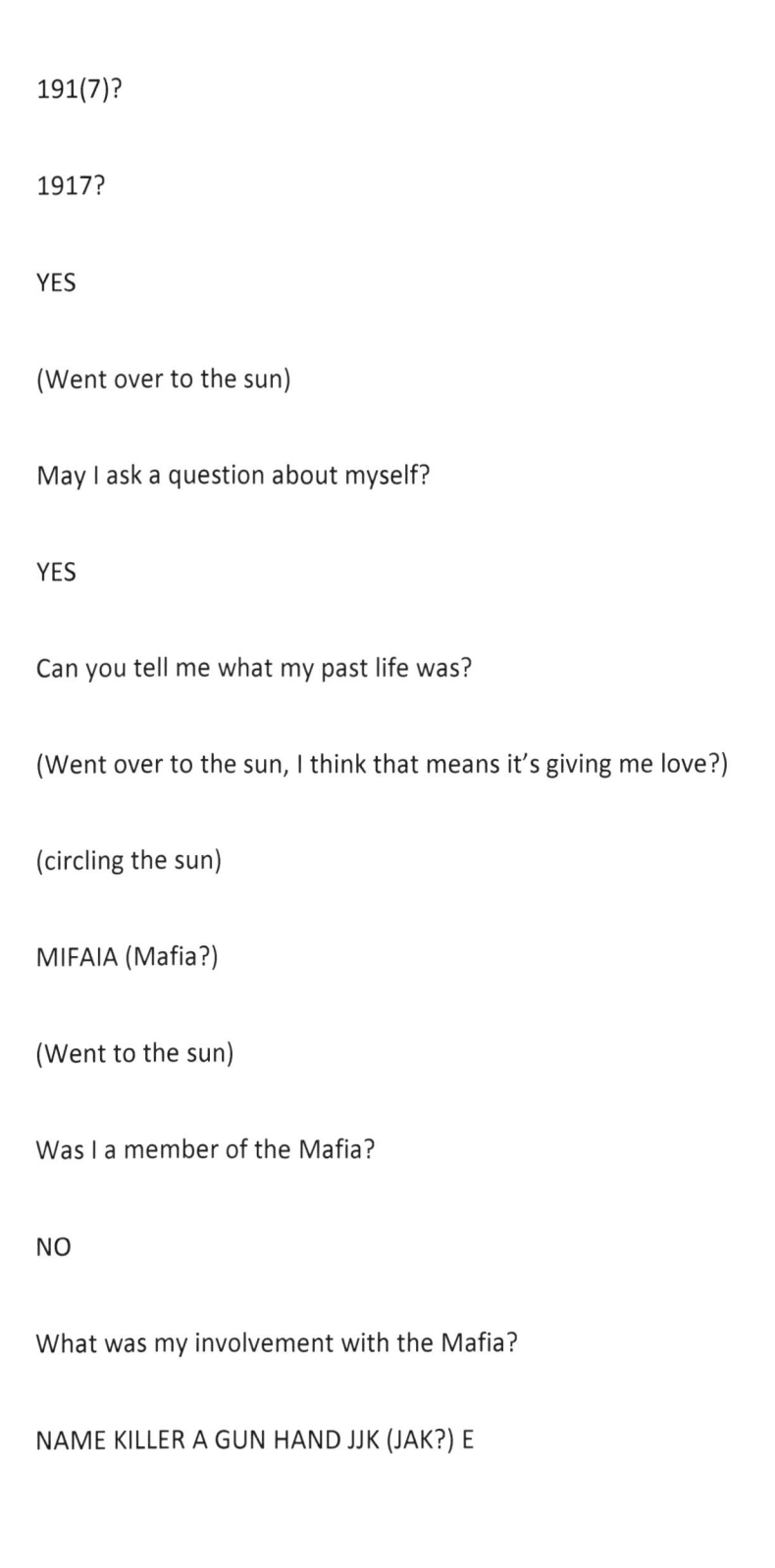

1917?

YES

(Went over to the sun)

May I ask a question about myself?

YES

Can you tell me what my past life was?

(Went over to the sun, I think that means it's giving me love?)

(circling the sun)

MIFAIA (Mafia?)

(Went to the sun)

Was I a member of the Mafia?

NO

What was my involvement with the Mafia?

NAME KILLER A GUN HAND JJK (JAK?) E

(Jake?)

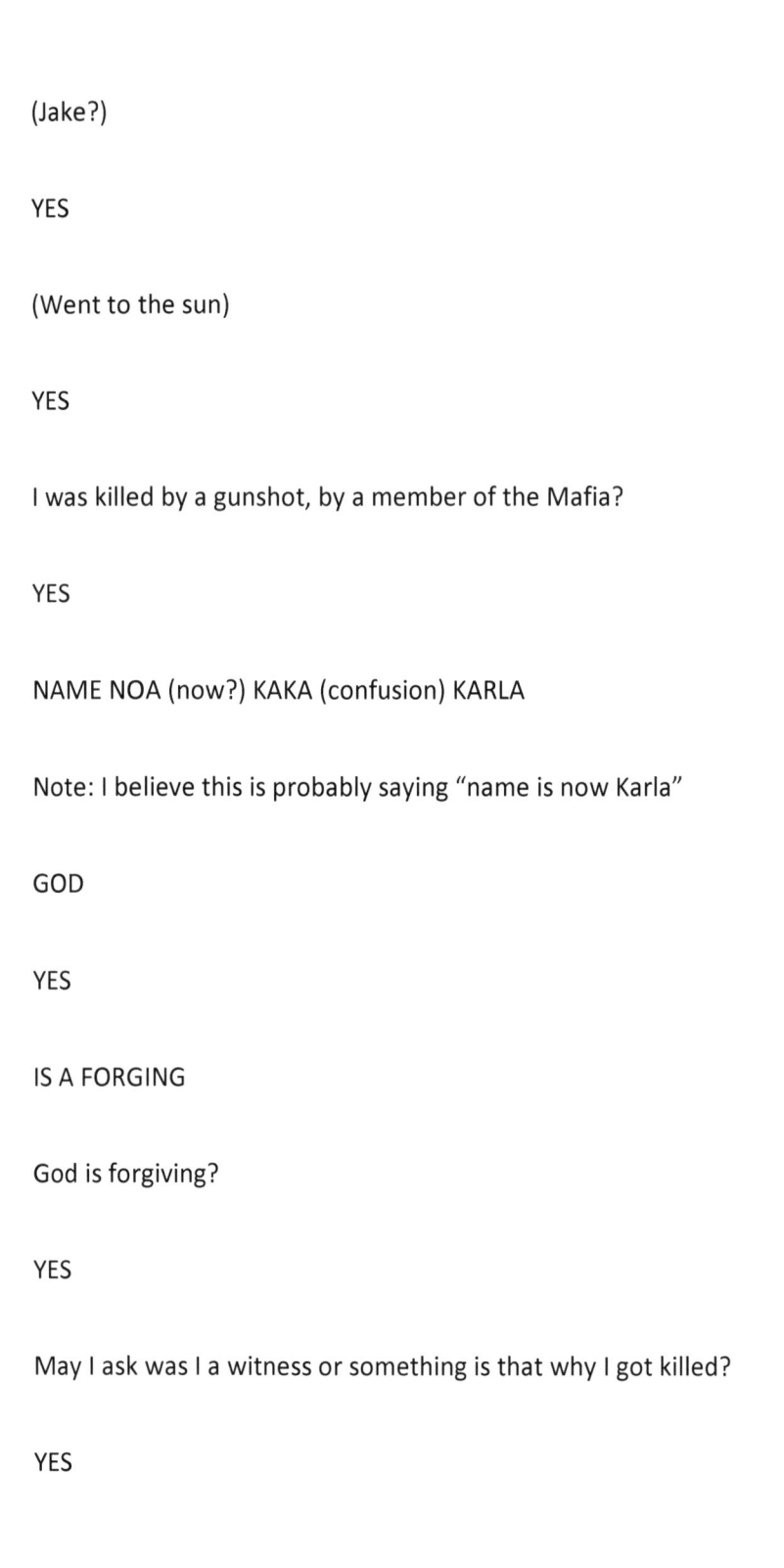

YES

(Went to the sun)

YES

I was killed by a gunshot, by a member of the Mafia?

YES

NAME NOA (now?) KAKA (confusion) KARLA

Note: I believe this is probably saying "name is now Karla"

GOD

YES

IS A FORGING

God is forgiving?

YES

May I ask was I a witness or something is that why I got killed?

YES

May I ask what year it was when I died?

1919

1919?

NO

Can you tell me please?

1929

1929, is that correct?

YES

May I ask what city it was I died in?

TAB (A or B)SEIA

Taboseia?

YES

YOTOUHNB

Was this an European country?

NO

TGIOGAUIRA

Is this a name of a state in the US?

YES

(Went to the sun)

Is this Georgia, the state of Georgia?

Note: I don't know if this is true, I think I was just getting gibberish or they couldn't tell me for some reason

YES

Ededena, it's almost time for me to go to bed, do you have any final messages for me?

YES

What is that message?

JUST LOVE YOURSELF

Just love yourself

NOBHC JANUARY ALL (or M) OBSESSTINHALUAL

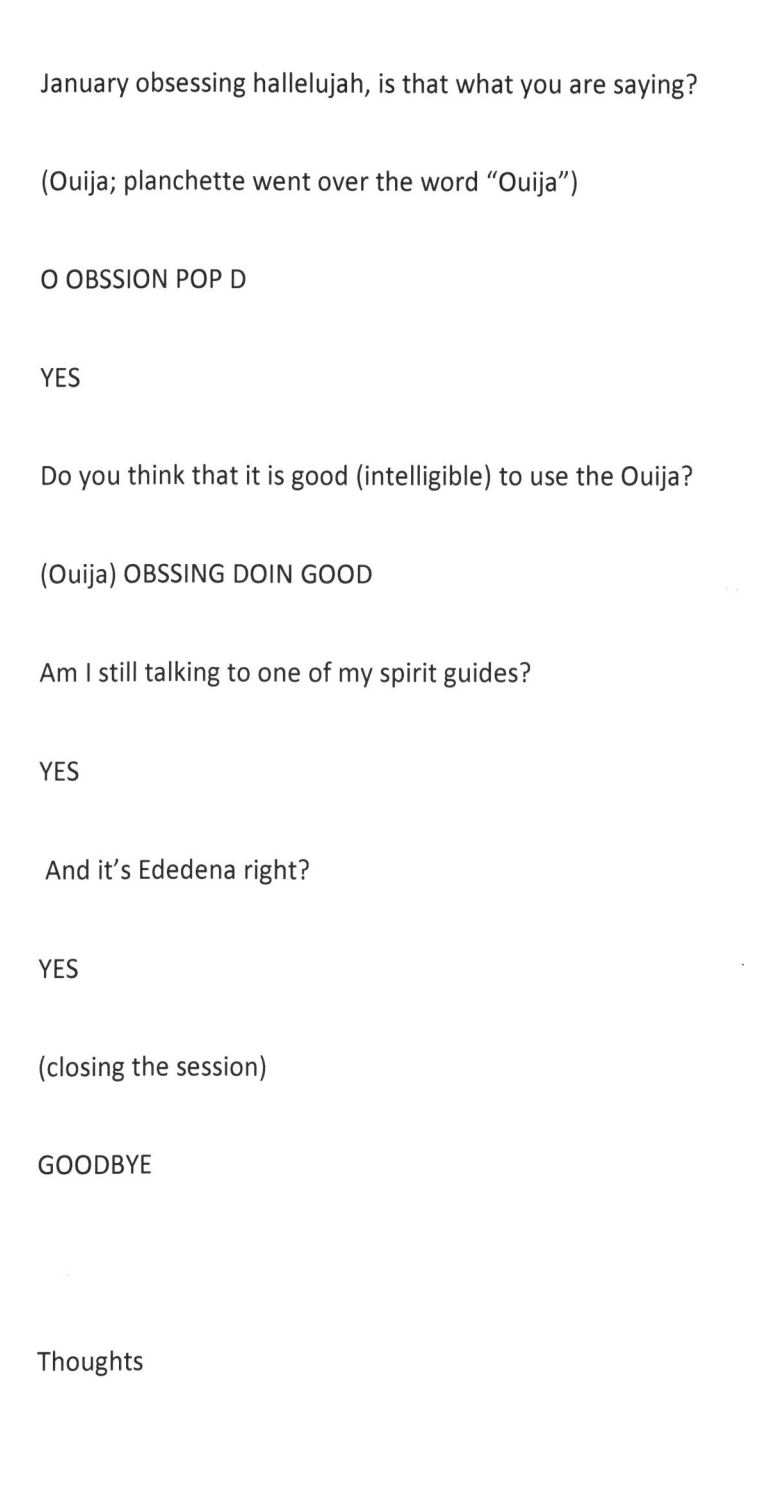

January obsessing hallelujah, is that what you are saying?

(Ouija; planchette went over the word "Ouija")

O OBSSION POP D

YES

Do you think that it is good (intelligible) to use the Ouija?

(Ouija) OBSSING DOIN GOOD

Am I still talking to one of my spirit guides?

YES

And it's Ededena right?

YES

(closing the session)

GOODBYE

Thoughts

Ededena, or Dena or Dean is trying to tell me to quit smoking and eat healthy, I also get the message that God is good. Also to love myself as well as Ouija is a good public (?!) tool. The planchette has gone over the word Ouija a few times so I think there is a message there. I asked about my past life and he said I was killed by a member of the Mafia or perhaps some sort of gang, by a gunshot wound in the year 1929. I wasn't able to get the name of the city or country or state as either they didn't know or wasn't allowed to tell me. I'll probably try to get it clarified at the next session. Also my name was probably Jake. Possibly I was a witness to a crime and was killed for it. He reiterates that God is forgiving, perhaps I did some sort of crime?

The planchette kept going over to the word Ouija on the board and I asked about it, the message wasn't clear but something about obsessing and doing good with it, maybe? The messages still aren't clear and I need to meditate more and let it flow.

Next time:

Request to talk to spirit guide DENA or DEAN

Clarify city and place of death in past life

Clarify about using the Ouija, there seems to be a message there. "

~Elm Ouija 2015

What an amazing and uplifting session she had! This is all possible for you as well. All you have to do is open your mind to the positive side of the Ouija and low and behold! There is a 100% different side to this coin and you too will experience this.

Chapter 6

Miscellaneous Ouija Musings

Throughout this chapter I will be giving you even more amazing stories all in association with the board. I hope for you as a reader find this book to be a guide book to using the board. In hopes of the best communications for all of you.

A Very Random Thought Bubble (Higher-Self Maybe) ?

I always warn people of the dangers that accompany the Ouija Board. I would never advise anyone with any sort of health issue to use the board. Staying away from street and recreational drugs, are a plus too, also illegal. I've always used my board in a " clean " way. I would never want to ruin the connections I have with this parallel universe.

In a sense of " knowing " you feel so much peace, you don't need narcotics to feel great. It's all coming from within your own self. This is your higher-self, now, telling you this. You don't need a life-style like that which you fear.

Never let those horrible, destructive things in your life. They will take your light away from you. If you have no light you can't shine. It's the truth, it's real, it's common sense.

Balancing yourself and attuning with these energies, sober, is a sure way to make good and clear communications.

Go outside right now, barefoot, cold or hot, day or not. Earth yourself and feel everything connecting to the nerves of your feet.

4/22/2015

This book has not only helped me heal myself, but ones around me are healing as well. They tell me their Dream Encounters ". It's bizarre, my " spell-craft " work is present in their dreams.

All in all here is my book review, my first, too. A very well written and amazing piece of literature. Thank You Karen. :)

Coexisting and Coping With The Dead

Death is inevitable. We live it, breathe it, go through it. Only in accepting your own death you will most certainly, then be able to fully appreciate your own existence. I feel as if Necromancy is a way of life. Incorporating death into most aspects of your life. It happens and we have to deal with it. Nothing can be destroyed, energy just changes forms. That can be scientifically backed too. The Ouija and a lot of divination techniques can't be. Though these methods work for us. Being shy of 20 years using the Talking Board, you'd think one would know.

I'm not sure if I'm looking for scientific proof, although it helps. The idea of Quantum Physics gives me a much better feeling. There's more depth and works to study, on Death. It is afterall the only thing promised. I do believe in a Higher Power, just not sure what to call it/label/put a face on. I feel personally the dead are much more readily accessible to us.

I see Death in my Craft and in all aspects of my life, I've embraced it, I do not fear it. I don't want it to happen anytime soon, nor wish it on anything or anyone. So my thought is, the Ouija is a tool that proves useful and effective in it's use. Seeing the dead and spirits, energies, what have you, helps with using the board.

I never asked to see such beings. Over the years I've learned to let it work on my behalf, instead of become a burden or bother. It can be tough being a sensitive and clairvoyant. The dead surround us at all times. The air we breathe, the winds, oceans. Meditation and studying is what's kept me balanced.

I wasn't always balanced. That just lead to a reckless lifestyle and choice of acquaintances. I see a lot of sensitives that turn to opiates and narcotic abuse, it's a sad thing too. Don't use a pill to numb it away. It will work for you eventually. When I was unbalanced I turned to pain killers a lot. I overcame that though, until this day. The spirits I believe (my grandma mostly) helped me through it.

It can be a great tool for self exploration and mind solving problems. Explore it. ;)

Being sensitive and in a house that has activity, is tiring. Sleep aid does help lol. Sadly but truly it does. They do keep me up tonight though, even through sleep aid. Always know who's alive and who's not.

Egg Cleansing: How to. (Cleansing with an egg)

I'm almost certain that the egg cleansing is of Hispanic heritage. Eggs are a great way of cleansing yourself of negative energy. It's simple, fast and it works.

What you need is 1 egg at room temperature and a glass of water. I use a fancy wine glass because I'm silly like that. You can say any prayers you like while doing the egg cleansing. For some odd reason I'm stuck on making the sign of the cross on my forehead with the egg. This being said, it's probably a chain of the Catholic faith that hasn't been snipped from my brain. Do what you feel is right tho.

Starting at the top of your head, going DOWNWARD only, swipe the egg down your entire body. Push the negative energy into that egg. Get the nap of your neck, hands and feet realy well. Once your done, crack the egg in the glass of water.

If you know how to read an egg by all means do so. The bubbles represent spirit taking care of the matter. Cleansing you of negative energy. That's the extent of my egg readings ;) Once your done, flush it down the toilet or throw the egg into a flowing stream of water.

You can do this as many times as you wish. You can light a white candle and use some sage also.

Crafting Your Own Reversible Candle

Most of today's candles are quite expensive! Not all of us can afford to buy a candle for $10-$20, wait for it to get shipped, or even find an Occult store near you. So here is my own recipe for crafting your own reversible candle. It'll cost you about $1.50 ... can't beat that huh?

Supplies You Will Need

1 white Seven Day Vigil candle (You can get these at the dollar store)

13 drops of Clearance Oil

13 Drops of Glow of Attraction Oil

A few drops of your own Blood

A birchwood stick for making the holes (you can get these for about 60 cents at Sally Beauty Supply)... a screw driver will work.

1 Sanitized needle to prick your finger

Alcohol wipes

If for any reason you are UNABLE to obtain the oils listed above simply use a few drops of your own blood or Saliva! I used the Glow of attraction oil to put a glow around myself, from future psychic attacks. Your blood is life, your blood carries your intent.

So on my own candle all I did was prepare it in my style. Going slightly into trance, making my intent very clear and focused my will (energy) into the candle. I then made the holes for the oils.

You can use construction paper or a black sharpie to draw the above image on your candle. Get creative as you like... This is YOUR candle.

There are certain Psalms that go along with the Reversible Candle, I don't say them, I'm not a Christian so I do not need it. You can either let your candle burn or say any set of prayers you'd like.

Now guess what..... You'r candle is finished. ;) I'd love to see your finished products! If you'd like them featured on here or on my Facebook Public Page, send me a line and I'd be more than happy to share your art.

Happy Crafting guy's N' gal's !

Necromancy Incense (How To)

Here is a very simple recipe for some very effective, Necromancy Incense. I created this about a year or so ago, the results are amazing! So, what you will need....

Copal Resin

Patchouli Oil

3 Red Rose Petals

a few drops of your own blood

A dash of Graveyard Dirt

Make sure you grind up your Copal resin into a very fine powder. This is going to act as the base and keep your incense burning. It does become quite clumpy, just keep grinding in the mortar and pestle. Once all your dry ingredients are evenly and well ground, add a drop of your own blood and a drop of the patchouli oil. Grind it up some more. It's a good idea to let it set out for about an hour, in a dry space. This way the oil and blood can actually have a short period to dry out a bit. With the intent of necromancy in mind, direct and focus all your energy into the mixture. You can use other techniques as you see fit. The dreams and visions this incense produces are phenomenal as well.

Creating a Spirit Vessel (Within a Luciferian Context)

Creating a Spirit Vessel requires a lot of astral work, visualization and time. To create an Ancestor Vessel, I will give this outline so that you can use it for more than just your Ancestors. Never bind your Ancestors to ANYTHING, it's just rude. So, you will need

A vessel of some sort (glass, wooden, Etc..)

You're going to want to wash it really well! Let it set outside in the sun for 3 days (if possible), so it can dry. Leave it in a window sill if you are unable to let it set outside due to weather or what not. Once your vessel has dried thoroughly in the sun, decorate it. An Ancestor Vessel will have all the symbols of death. Skulls, sigils for Saturn and Mercury, Certain seals of solomon, Etc.

Once you've decorated your Vessel now comes the Nganga. Some will say you CANNOT create an Nganga by yourself, I disagree. I've made one and it works amazing. I used a mini resin skull, for my Nganga, in this Ancestor Vessel. Place on the bottom of the vessel a small amount of cemetery dirt, twigs/stones from the cemetery, cemetery dirt from the graves of your Ancestors (always be respectful when taking the dirt, leave a few pennies, a cigarette or some water for them.) Now place any objects inside the vessel that you associate with your Ancestors (or whichever Spirit/Demon you are working with).

Now that it's all said and done, go into a meditative state, the death current, slow breathing techniques work great to get you there. Please do not use any sort of ethogen to achieve this state of being. Once you're in the astral state, call out to the shades of the dead, your Ancestors, the spirit you are creating the vessel for. Explain to them what you are doing. Be EXACT! Keeping your vessel on the triangle of arte, you are conjuring this energy into existence. So, now you have your vessel made, you've contacted the spiritual world, you'll get a gut feeling if it's " ok " to go ahead with your procedure.

Here comes the " Circle of The Dead " which will bind you to your Vessel.

Toss a small amount of gravel soil and a small amount of your own blood on top of your pre-created Nganga, that was placed inside your spirit vessel. Make sure you have this on your Triangle of Arte. Take your wand with your left hand, going counter clockwise around your vessel and intone the following :

" I summon the mighty dead from the spaces of silence from which the grave cradles. I give you life by blood and by soil, by the essence of my being. Emerge from your sleep of death and encircle my being, protecting my body as I dream and walk the web of night. As Thanatos I require your service, for we are bound by the laws of death "

The shade will now feed on your Astral body as you sleep, giving it nourishment to perform the duties of it's creation. The shades are forced away once you return back to your body/wake up.

These are very intense and time consuming procedures. It takes quite a bit of time to get to the state of mind you need to be in, to contact these beings. Take your time, research, read, learn. Always be safe, if you're not comfortable with it, don't do it. You can also pick up a copy of " The Book of The Witch's Moon " By Michael Ford.

Witch Bottles " Protecting Home and Land "

For this Witch Bottle you will need the following;

1. a small bottle or vial

2. Crushed mint

3. Crushed sage

4. dirt from the four corners of your land

5. a STERILE needle (for a small drop of your own blood)

6. Hekate Oil

7. Red String

8. wax of some sort (white)

Hallow your compass with the intent of bringing in all beneficial and positive energies, to help shield and protect your home/land, from any type of negativity. Since this is Traditional Witchcraft, you get a LOT more room for creativity, so get creative! Let spirit move you. Once you're in the frame of mind, at ease, peaceful, make your compass grow to engulf your entire house/land. See it, like a blown bubble, the iridescent colors they create.

You can come up with a Rhyme or chant to accompany this spell. Once you've focused your will, have your intent set, charge all your herbs and all other working materials. Fill up your bottle or vial with your herbs, a small prick of your finger, a small drop of your own blood, 3 drops of Hekate oil (optional). Put your cap on, or just wax it shut. Tie the red string counter-clockwise to invite beneficial energies in, protecting you, your loved ones, your land, from all harm and dangers, as well as ill will. When you get to the point of about 2 inches of thread left, focus all your energy into that knot. Know it is done.

Simple, eh. ;) You can keep this on your altar, some bury them. I hung mine in a tree and it's still there. I refresh them about every 1-4 years when I feel they've run their courses. I don't suggest BANISHING any energy, it helped you, why punish it? Thank them, you are done. ;)

This can be used in any context; Health, Love, Passion, Power, Healing... Have fun and let me know if it works for you! Thank you to all who watch my videos too. It's a really fanfuckingtastic feeling. If I can help one person, make one friend, it's worth it.

Lodestone Magick (My How To)

Lodestone Magick

This is about the easiest working I've ever done. Thank you to all that contributed to my questions concerning working the Lodestone! For your own lodestone magick here is what you will need;

1 small dish

1 load stone (female... they are phallic shaped)

Tiny drop of whiskey

metal fillings

piece of brown bag paper (or any paper)

Small items such as coins to represent what you are attracting to yourself.

Sterilized needle

Metal fillings I found out in the garage. Make sure to cleanse them.

All I did was took some sage, cleansed all my items I was going to be working with. Set those aside for now. Next you want to program your lodestone with what you intend to attract. Most say it's wise to only give your lodestone 1 task, I gave mine 4. Talk to it like it's a living being, because it's just that! A living being.

Now drop a tiny bit of whiskey on your lodestone. (not too much, do not get it drunk). Next you'll want to write on that brown bag paper, that which you wish to attract to yourself. I took a sterilized needle, a small prick of the ring finger, dapped it in each of the corners of the paper. I folded the paper towards myself, because we are bringing these things to us. I then charged the paper in the same manner as the lodestone.

Place your piece of paper in your dish, place the lodestone on top, and any other representations of what you are attracting, in with the lodestone. You can pray over this, I don't pray so I just speak to it every night, telling it how grateful I am for the work it's doing for me. Now take your metal fillings, or magnetic sand if you have it and put a VERY SMALL amount on top of it. This is feeding your lodestone.

You're all set! Now every night you're going to want to pray or talk to the stone itself. Envision those things that you are attracting with focused will. Once a week you will want to feed it to keep it going. Just give it a small pinch of your magnetic fillings or sand.

Personally, mine is working FANTASTIC! If you try this, let me know how it goes for you! Here is a video as well, showing my lodestone and explaining it in detail. Happy Attracting!

Luciferian Banishing Ritual

This is a great way to clear your mind before and after any rite. It also banishes any negativity in your body and from your space. A Basic before and after work.

Facing the altar, located in the east, take the athame and make the sign of the invoking pentagram, averse and envision a light emerge from your being.

" By the light of Lucifer, born of my desire for the attainment of becoming open to the gates of the dead to protect my very being, spirit and flesh.

Noctifer Observe ! "

Touch your forehead and recite:

" Ateh " (unto thee)

1. Facing the North, make the sign of the invoking pentagram averse, and envision the graves of the earth opening forth and encircling you, protecting you from all outside forms.

" By the light of Azazel, who brought to man and woman the knowledge of the serpent, attend my being in the protection of the kin of Witchblood ! "

Touching the genitals recite:

" Malkuth " (The Kingdom)

2. Facing West, make the sign of the invoking pentagram averse, and envision the waters circling you, forming great tempests with serpents and dragons seeking to devour that which would attack you.

" By the call of Shemyaza may the hidden knowledge and protection be revealed. By the desire of my many forms shall be passed from the grave to life. "

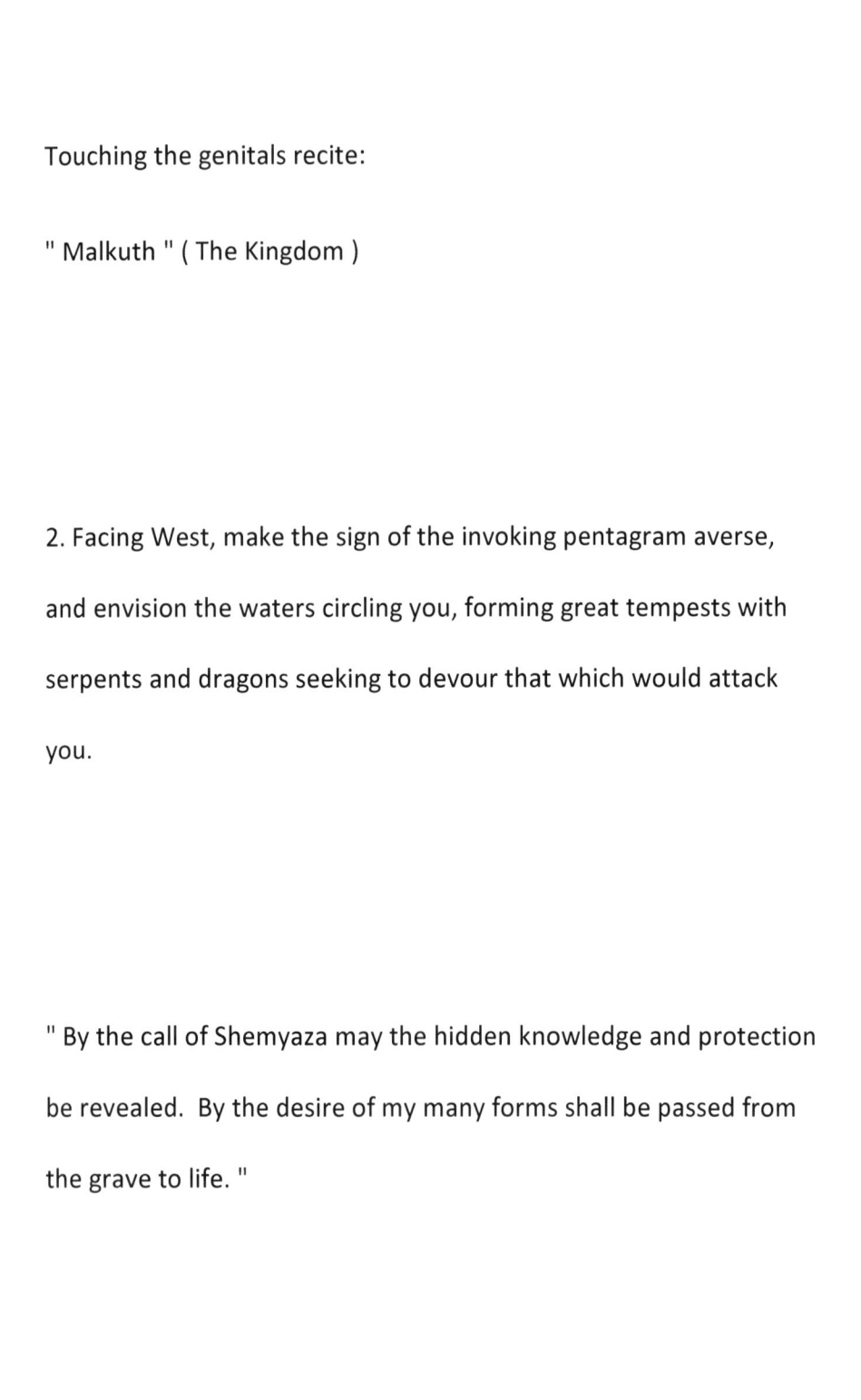

Touching the right shoulder recite:

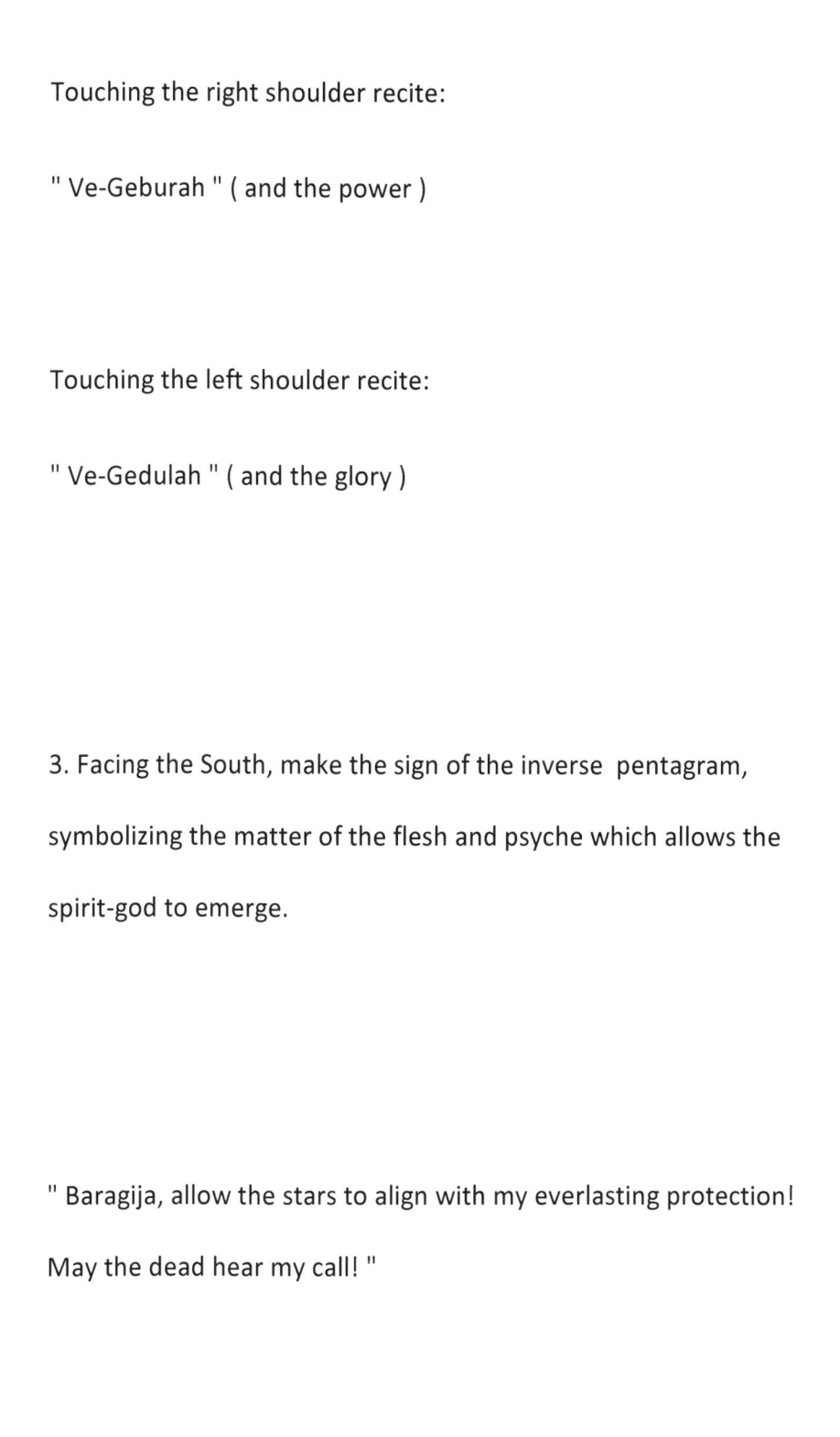

" Ve-Geburah " (and the power)

Touching the left shoulder recite:

" Ve-Gedulah " (and the glory)

3. Facing the South, make the sign of the inverse pentagram, symbolizing the matter of the flesh and psyche which allows the spirit-god to emerge.

" Baragija, allow the stars to align with my everlasting protection! May the dead hear my call! "

4. Face now the altar and recite:

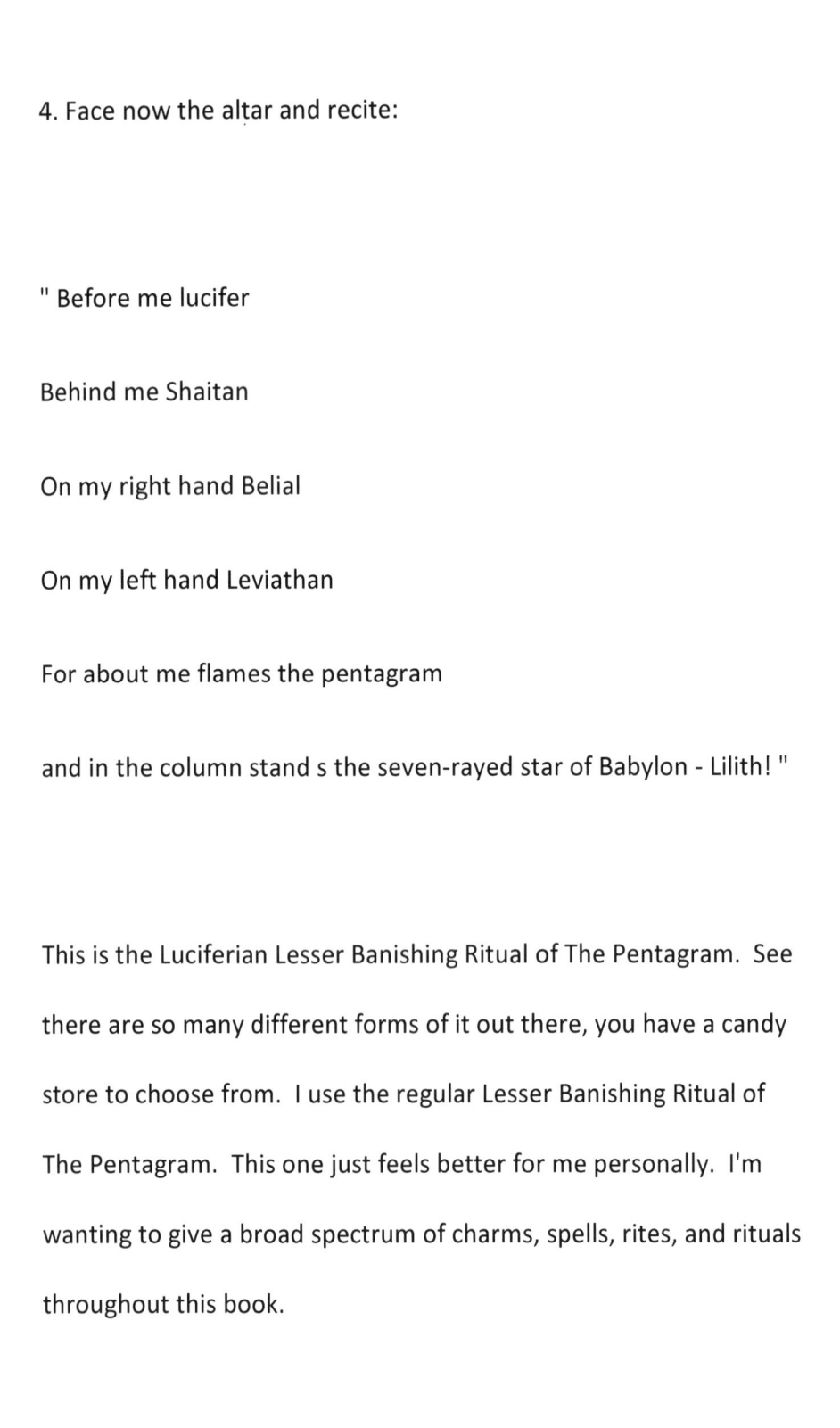

" Before me lucifer

Behind me Shaitan

On my right hand Belial

On my left hand Leviathan

For about me flames the pentagram

and in the column stand s the seven-rayed star of Babylon - Lilith! "

This is the Luciferian Lesser Banishing Ritual of The Pentagram. See there are so many different forms of it out there, you have a candy store to choose from. I use the regular Lesser Banishing Ritual of The Pentagram. This one just feels better for me personally. I'm wanting to give a broad spectrum of charms, spells, rites, and rituals throughout this book.

Charging a Fetish/Nganga

Already have a fetish/nganga made? PERFECT! Here is a simple way to charge and bring to life your fetish!

Facing the altar, take grave soil and toss a small amount onto the fetish/nganga. Now pour a small amount of your own blood into the fetish/nganga. Take your wand, encircling counter-clockwise, and intone:

" I summon the mighty (name of fetish) from the space of silence from which the outside cradles. I give you life by blood and by soil, by the essence of my being. Emerge from your realm and encircle my being, protecting my body as I dream and walk the web of night. Aid me in the art of magick, the left hand path. As Thanatos I require your service, for we are bound by the laws of death "

As you sleep you fetish's / ngangas will feed from your astral body. It's safe to say that they do not take enough energy from you, to make you physically ill, or cause any real damage.

Charging a Fetish (Mask Magick Outline)

My basic outline for crafting a mask to embody the archetypal energy of your chosen God or Goddess / Spirit / Angel / Demon /

Daemon. This is not set in stone, this is just my way of going about the mask magick process. I've chosen Pan's story as my archetypal energy to imbue the mask with the energy of Pan and that of his story, hence creating within myself / ourselves a merging of his consciousness into our own. I feel this to be a very transforming for oneself spiritually. The intent and purpose of crafting a mask and reenacting the Myth is to bring about an Alchemical change within your own psyche. Whichever myth you've chosen please be sure that's what type of energy that vibes with that of your own. Choose a God or Goddess, Spirit, Angel, or Daemon that is going to be of the most benefit to your transformation. I vibe very well with Pan's story. Being rejected by his father for being different and then becoming the God of the wild, the wild and free one, the trickster, jokester.

It is best to craft your mask with all hand made items. Paper mache, Plaster, etc... If you cannot do this for some reason then finding a blank mask and adding to it, crafting it, bending it to suit your need and shape it to that of the God or Goddess you've chosen will work just as fine. It's all in your intention. As for myself I will not mess with paper mache or plaster, so I must find a blank mask to add to it and imbue it with Pan's Story. Having picked a God or Goddess, find their story and study it, let the myth sink into your subconscious mind. For you can and will learn a lot about yourself through these myths and legends. Giving you the opportunity to embody that Archetypal energy (God) and transform you from the inside. When one puts on the mask and ritual garb you are becoming, inviting that God or Goddess, that energy inside of yourself. You become that God or Goddess while in an altered state of merging.

I have not chosen a specific moon phase nor am I following any type of astrological regimen. I am going by my own intuition and letting my Higher Self guide me along the way. I feel with this type of magick and spiritual transformation, using your intuition is going to be best to suit your personally. I am however performing all acts of mask magick within a Traditional Witchcraft outline and context. You do not have to do this, stick to your tradition and what makes YOU feel the most comfortable and most empowered. This is about YOU and transforming yourself, gaining knowledge, etc..

Once you've crafted your mask and it's completely finished you are going to need to charge your Fetish. Don't get me wrong you are going to want to charge it while you are crafting it as well. Play songs of the God or Goddess you've chosen. Listen to an audio book about the myths and legends surrounding the Archetypal energy you've chosen. Add items that are going to reflect the God or Goddess you are going to merge with. There is so much room for creativity while crafting your mask let your imagination go wild. Get yourself in that mood, set the ambiance, get in touch with that energy while crafting the mask.

After my mask is finished I will re-read Pan's Myth and let it sink it even that much more. Really getting a good grasp on the meaning of the story. How does it relate to you? To your Life, your inner struggles? What are you going to be changing and transforming? I will cast my compass counter clockwise inviting in any beneficial energies. From there I shall perform the invocation of the Witchmother and Witchfather. My compass has been laid and the proper energies invited in, the mask magick is ready to begin. Here is a simple technique that I've given in my most recent video (Charging A Fetish) you can use to charge and amp up the energy of your mask that much more. It's very simple, it's very easy and you need only two items. 1.) Your wand or blasting rod. 2.) Grave Soil. Lastly your mask, obviously.

Lay the mask down in front of your working space. Hold it high and proud, showing it to the God or Goddess you've chosen. Speak to that God/Goddess and explain in detail your reasons for crafting this mask. Really have a good conversation with your energy you are working with. When you are ready take up a small bit of the Grave Soil and sprinkle it on the mask. Take your wand, going counter clockwise around the mask, sending that energy, blasting it into the mask you. You can add a drop of your own blood to the mask (completely optional). Now you are going to intone the following chant/charm for charging the Fetish.

" I summon the mighty (Name of God/Goddess) from the spaces of silence from which the outside cradles. I give you life by blood and by soil, by the essence of my being. Emerge from your realm and encircle my being, protecting my body as I dream and walk the web of night. Aid me in the art of Magick, the left hand path. As Thanatos I require your service, for we are bound by the laws of birth and death ".

At this time you should be feeling the energy within your compass, within your body, the God or Goddess should be present. After you've charged your Fetish, your mask, place the mask on your face. You can reenact the chosen myth if you wish or you can just sit in silent meditation and let the mask transform you. Let yourself become the embodiment of the God or Goddess. For myself I shall be playing the panpipes and drumming, any type of woodland instruments that will bring forth the energy of Pan into my compass, my being. You can really turn this into a play if you will. Going all out with other ritual attire to bring that energy into your being. You may experience unusual thoughts, movements, words or actions. Make sure to set an intent to remember each thing that happens during your reenactment, if you trance out like I often do.

When you feel you are finished reenacting the myth or rite of the chosen God/Goddess let your senses calm down. Let yourself come back into your being becoming fully aware and conscious. Many traditions have cake and ale. In Traditional Witchcraft we have the red meal. The red meal is something I will be performing as a " thanksgiving " after the rite / ritual reenactment itself. You may now close down your working space. Thank all the energies that you have worked with in your compass. Thank the God/Goddess for attending your rite. Sweep away your compass or draw the energy back into yourself and give it back to the universe. Now you are going to want to find a very special place for your mask. Keep it put up, or on display for all to see while you are not working with it. When you feel a time has come and you need to reenact that myth/rite again for further transformation or just to get in touch with that Divine spark do your entire ritual once again. This time you won't have to charge the mask with the " Charging of the Fetish ".

Keep a journal separate from other journals. Use this one specifically for your mask magick ventures. Write down anything you've seen, felt, smelt, sensed, while doing the reenactment. Go back through your mask magick journal and see how you have progressed. Have you changed anything within yourself for the better? Have you overcome any obstacles in your path? What exactly has the mask done for you? Maybe you just simply want to connect and become one with your chosen being. Whatever the purpose/intent of your mask magick rite, always know it's a very special act and a very sacred one. You are taking on the personification of that energy you have invoked within that mask. Hence you always treat it with the utmost respect.

I hope this general outline and a little more explanation on the subject sheds light for you, helps you to transform and become closer to your own divine spark. Enjoy your mask, enjoy the dance, enjoy the song!

ZoZo: A Case of Mass Hysteria

So we have all heard the tired tale of " ZoZo The Ouija Board Demon ", but do you know the origins of this supposed demon?

What I am about to tell you is my theory and my theory only. The opinions expressed in this article are that of my own and are not that of other ZoZo researchers. I have recently came to my own conclusion on what exactly this Phenomenon is and where it stems. Lets find out more shall we?

The letter " Z " in many cultures, is considered to be " evil " or " taboo ", for reasons unknown to me and many others. In Africa we have the " Zu " people which are highly religious and spiritual people. My best guess would be that the " Zu " people(s) have gotten it right. Within the faith of Vodou we have the letter "Z" quite often and it is not a " Taboo " or " evil " letter. We find it in Veve's (symbols for the spirits), and then we find that the Gede Spirits use the term " ZoZo " to refer to their batons, as a penis, while ritually dancing.

Now within ceremonial Magick, Sigil Magick, Planetary Magick, The Goetia, Necromancy, The blossoming of the Spiritualist movement in the 1800's we see a plethora of seals, sigils, and signatures that do in fact contain many " Z's " as well as the actual name ZoSo, not " ZoZo. The earliest known Signature for the Planet Saturn comes from the 1500's, right out of the " Red Dragon " also called " The Grand Grimoire ". It was only until the usage of the Ouija Board became popular again that this thought form or " perversion " of the Gods of Saturn, better known as " ZoZo " began surfacing the board.

Now I personally see " ZoZo " as a tupla, a thought form, something that has been given form by one person and released into the cosmos. Since " ZoZo's " character is very rude, hateful, spiteful, and child-like. That specific entity is the embodiment of all things negative or " evil ". " ZoZo " promotes domestic violence, alcoholism, drug usage and very bizarre acts. You can read the stories for yourself of how he will surface a board, make sexual advances towards women and even men. He will curse you out and yet sometimes he will be quite kind. Does this sound like something we may all know?

I see so many stories of " possession " tales attributed to " ZoZo ". I see so many people complain and say they cannot get rid of this " demon ". Well, what is a demon actually? First Demon is Latin for " Helpful Spirit ". Demons were never actual demons, they were earthly helpers to mankind. As humans have both good and bad inside themselves so does the Demon or Spirit. Some are not all good and some are not all bad, a lot of them you will find to be very neutral.

To put the cases of " Possession " to rest here is my explanation for this. Mainly teenagers are going to want to contact such a being of hatred and violence, for they want to be scared. The majority of people that contact this entity WANT to be scared and WANT the fear. They hear the stories via the grand old internet, get a Ouija and start to make a mockery of the board and the use of the board. The spiritual usage of the board itself, as it is not a game or a toy, it is a tool and you use it, you do not play with it.

With all the hype and adrenaline coursing through their blood, naturally, they are going to have self-fulfilling prophecies. This is when someone believes something so much that it becomes their reality. Hence The " Ouija Board Demon ZoZo " manifests out of this hysteria. I find it a very easy way to scapegoat. I see many articles on the internet these days placing blame for the neighbors cat dieing. Maybe this is one way for these people to lash out and express emotions and actions they would not be able to get away with in their right minds, so, scapegoating their own actions and saying " ZoZo had control ".

I find this very silly. We were all born with free will. Now I am not a Christian at all and I do not hold any beliefs of Christianity. God is not going to interfere with your free will. " Satan " or " ZoZo " is not and CANNOT interfere with your own free will. Why? Because it is free will and it is your own free will. Now if you are weak enough and believe and fall for this fake being, then you are receiving what you have been conditioned by, via the internet and other sources on the subject of " ZoZo ".

Modern Psychology tells us that when someone puts enough thought into something, enough energy behind it that it can physically manifest for those individuals. The ones that spread the message of " ZoZo " and continue to feed his existence are the ones that condition others and project that thought form onto the rest of the human community. It is rather quite simple. Think of it as the Salem Witch Trials. A tiny bit of bad wheat and the mold produced mass hysteria, delusions, hallucinations, accusations of Witchcraft, Spirit possession, the list goes on.

This is my firm belief that " ZoZo " is in fact a thought form, created by one person, fed by thousands and continues to grow and take form and shape. It is and one day will be just another Urban Legend such as Slender Man and Bloody Mary. I actually have more faith that Bloody Mary exists than I do " ZoZo ". Now am I saying that everyone who has written a book on " ZoZo " or experiences this being are liars? Not at all, not in the least! I believe that these people are obsessed with the idea and therefore they simply condition themselves to believe it. The rational mind isn't thinking properly. The realm of imagination is active and very strong.

Now for some facts on the topic. ZoSo for one is not a word it is a symbol. ZoSo is Jimmy Page's own symbol of Saturn and Capricorn, his astrological signs. ZoSo is also the signature of Saturn. So below is a picture of the sigil of Saturn (ZoSo) and it's first appearance in " The Red Dragon ".

Now you can see that ZoSo is in reference to Saturn. Nothing more and nothing less. symbol = Saturn (ruler of Capricorn astrology sign)The French text simply says that "Saturn rules over the lives of mankind, extending or terminating it and making life happy or painful". Pretty interesting stuff isn't it?

So seeing has how Chronos, Titan, and Zeus are all in relation to Saturn do you see the similarities? If you were constantly being portrayed as an evil, malicious being, would you get a little upset at times? I know I surely would. So think about this. When you are using the Ouija and you have ill intentions, you are using it while drinking, you do not have a stable spiritual foundation to go off of, and base your Ouija Sessions on those emotions and imbalances what do you think you are going to get? Exactly what you brought with you to the table.

Human projection or the projection of a thought (basically brain-washing) people into believing in this being is what I feel is the true issue at hand. It is our brains that make us seek out even more answers to questions without any real evidence of the existence of

" ZoZo ". Sure people claim this " demon " is real but where is the proof? The only proof we really have are speculations. Within the realm of possibilities you can alchemically transform this negative entity " ZoZo " into something amazing. Something better than what you think " ZoZo " is. If you are faced with this being just remember in Freddy. Nancy turns her back on him and takes back every ounce of power she gave him and he went away. This my friends is what " ZoZo " is.

Saturn is also a very tricky planet! So when contacting Saturn be sure to be very literal for Saturn IS very literal. Saturnus will help you with your problems yet at the same time make you face obstacles to overcome those problems. If you are not being true to yourself Saturn will bring this out. Saturn will bring out so many things inside of you, which is what I would call " Inner Demons ".

Some of Saturn's related deities are as follows: Ah Puch, Ahriman, Asrael, Erebos, Hekate, HodrItzcolihuqui, Mokoi, Moros, Sebek, Sedna, Set, Skadi. Saturn also rules Saturday. Saturn is the planet of manifestation, Magickal Manifestation at that!

" Like Jupiter, Saturn has an intricate Moon system, with ten Moons in all. It's largest Moon, Titan, is the size of Mercury. As Jupiter is second only to the Sun in gravitational power, Saturn is second only to Jupiter, making it a "heavy weight" in terms of spiritual power. Like Jupiter, Saturn is a spiritual teacher. Jupiter is expansion to Saturn's power of contractions. They are the first of the spiritual planets, or the upper octaves of the personal planets. Saturn is considered the upper octave of the Moon, both tied together through the concept of karma. The symbol of Saturn is a cross on top of a crescent Moon.

Spiritually, Saturn is associated with both the root chakra and the crown. As the ruler of the root, Saturn relates the earth element, the physical world and all the trials and limitations that come with being in the world. As the ruler of the crown, Saturn represents the resolution of karma, and the move into higher consciousness. Saturn is the teacher, but unlike Jupiter, it is a taskmaster teacher.

When you listen to it, everything is fine. When you don't, Saturn manifests whatever you are ignoring in your life, usually as a challenge that you are forced to face. The metal of Saturn is traditionally lead, because it represents the weight of the responsibilities we carry.

Magically, Saturn is the power of manifestation. It brings things into form, both our karma and our intentions, if they match our spiritual path. Saturn is the master of discipline, named after the Roman version of the Greek Chronos, the Titan associated with the harvest and reaping both rewards and consequences. Saturn is often like our Father Time and Grim Reaper archetype mixed into one. In the Kabalah, Saturn is associated with the sephiroth of Binah, and linked to the divine feminine, cosmic goddess and destroyer. Saturn is the power of the primal and ancient ones in any culture – the first gods, the Ancient Father and Mother. " BY: CHRISTOPHER PENCZAK

So the above description of Saturn and its magickal correspondences, deities, plants and stones gives us a lot more insight into the truth behind " ZoZo ". The black bird associated with " ZoZo " is also a very sacred bird. Sacred to The Goddess, The

God Odin, and many other deities. Some say that the crow is " bad luck " or " an evil omen " I say that is just superstition. So in conclusion " ZoZo " had to have been made up by SOMEONE. It has to have come from somewhere. I personally think it is ZoSo being twisted and manipulated to fit the needs of the " ZoZo Seekers ".

Again these are my theories and mine only. So I ask you to research for yourself. Seek out what you feel is right. Do not let human conditioning and human projection influence you to the point that you torture yourself over a false " demon ".

Dead Johnny Cracked Corn -and We Got Scared-

There was so much to do in our " village " growing up. Literally it is a village and still is to this day. The Indians actually settled here first and then were demolished by the greedy men that thought they were better than the " primitive heathens ". Sadly, all the Indians from this small Village are no longer in the area. They did name this " village " which I will not name in this blog. You can say we are literally living in the center of " the woods ", on the outskirts of the city. A very fascinating place to live. Having so much land to roam and explore. I truly believe we did see the Wee Ones in the woodlands, nymphs, gnomes, faeries, all of these other-worldly creatures. This is when Pan was even more heavily into the picture (for myself anyways). My best friend had chosen the " Fairy Path " as she called it. She was fascinated by the Wee Ones as was I. I still felt more drawn to the primal energies, the raw, the darker, the old Gods.

Often times we'd build ELABORATE " forts " made of tree bark, sticks, moss and hay. We were so creative and imaginative we had about 10 of these " forts " throughout the entire " village ". We'd even go out of our way and plant flowers, create stone walk ways in the many different woodland areas in our " village ". Now that I look back at it I can say it would look something like you'd see from The Wizard of Oz. Those small huts with grass tops, hay sticking out, tiny windows and tiny doors. We were very tiny after all, we were only kids. So you can use your imagination on that one. The visions I am recalling are quite astonishing and beautiful. I do believe that we had " awoke " quite a few things within our " village " back in our younger days. Now living further away from the " village ", moving into a farm house/used to be an old school house/children of the corn, was quite refreshing and new. Being away from neighbors, or at least having one to two neighbors about 3 miles apart from me is so much better for my practices.

The history of our small " Village " is rather quite interesting! I'll go further into detail at a latter time. Returning back to the old grain shaft, drawing the Pentagrams in chalk, " pretending " to summon spirits, holding seances as kids do. One DAY, now mind you this was in pure daylight. We're exploring some of the other silos that surrounded the grain mill. Now this could have been our imagination or we unknowingly did summon a spirit that was a resident of this " village ". Roaming around inside these giant aluminum barns, playing in the hay, admiring the pitch forks and the old farm equipment we kept hearing something walk behind us. We'd take a step and feel " it " take a step RIGHT along with us. Ok, so this sort of " spooked " us in a way. Having grown up watching Freddy from the age of 2 and Halloween nothing really scared us too much, not like this.

We actually started to get pretty spooked, we spooked ourselves letting our imaginations run wild. Now this is where I have no idea what came, where it came from or what it was. Still roaming around and exploring these "new" things we'd never seen before, I picked up a beautiful machete. My " Best friend " was right beside me and she was in awe of the beauty of this thing. That very second we heard a very quiet voice. It was the voice of an old man " please leave". I looked at her and she looked at me. We were both puzzled. I said " fuck it ! Let's keep exploring ". She agreed and we went on our merry way! We got to the end of the long silo now looking at the machete in the light. More foot steps were heard behind us. This time I thought someone was fucking with us so we both turned around, ready to shank just about anybody that was even about to hurt us. To our surprise, standing RIGHT in front of us was this old man. His clothes were that of an old farmer, from the 1800's or so. He was as white as my hair, as white as the clouds! I looked at my " best friend " and whispered to her " we should..... ".... I stopped. I couldn't even talk. It felt like something was literally taking the air out from our lungs and not permitting us to talk.

Still staring at this man, scary as hell, well now that I look back at it, he wasn't actually scary, just a bit different, maybe a lost spirit? We both stood there looking at him in total shock. He looked right at us and very slowly, monotone voice he says " Please leave and do not come back here ". I looked over at my friend and we were suddenly able to talk and breathe again. I let out a loud " FUCK YOU!!! " as we busted ass back to our house. Turning around from time to time to see if he was still back there, he wasn't! This guy was NO WHERE to be seen. We went back again, looking for this " farmer " that had informed us to get out. Nothing, absolutely NOTHING! The thing that stuck out most to me personally was his overalls. They were a very sun-bleached / faded blue denim with dinghy white stripes.

Quite a few years later we had started to wonder about this mysterious " farmer " once again. Going back to the same spot, tracing our steps, doing the same things we did before. Still nothing! Not a sign of this man. We climbed up into the Elevator of the Grain Shaft and walked up to this door that read " office ". We picked the lock and walked in. There was a picture of the EXACT same man, hanging on the wall. Under neath of his photograph was his Date of birth...... followed by.... his DEATH. This spooked us big time. He had been a school teacher that was this small " village " previously had before the grain shaft was built and put in. The man in fact did die in the grain shaft, later on finding out that he was also a farmer and was very stern and protective over CHILDREN.

Why he told us to get out was beyond me and my " best friend ". We had no idea why he wanted us out of that place so badly. Now this is the astonishing part. About three years after that the building that we had been " hanging " around in had collapsed and killed one to two people. Was he warning us of an upcoming disaster? Was he actually protecting us? Or was it our subconscious minds projecting the images into the material world? To this day She and I will never know. If we were to have continued to mess around in that ONE specific silo we surely would have been CRUSHED and died instantly.

~ Abracadabra ~ Manifesting

Abracadabra is the Hebrew word for " invoking the aid of helpful spirits against disease, death, and misfortune. Used for curing ague and fevers as a charm bag. For illness you write ABRACADABRA on a piece of paper, I prefer parchment paper, any paper will do. You fold the paper into the shape of a cross, folding it AWAY from you, for you are repelling the illness or disease. You wear this small charm around your neck for 9 days. On the 9th day you're going to want to take the charm to a crossed roads or a running body of water, anywhere AWAY from your house. Toss the charm behind you and DO NOT look back.. You've just released your illness, sickness or disease within your body. Always make sure to FIRST and foremost get MEDICAL attention FIRST.

You can engrave this symbol on an inverted, white triangle stone.

ABRACADABRA = " It will be created in my words "

So for those of us that are going to be using this charm for reasons other than health, disease or sickness first decide upon the intent of your working. What is that you want to manifest? So we have our intent set for the spell/charm.

Now for me I won't do an entire ritual for this at all. I will simply set down in front of my altar, possibly light some candles for the Witchmother and Witchfather, I will however lay a compass round. I will also invite any beneficial energies in with me, like my ancestors for that extra boost. This is just a generalized outline of this spell.. You can do MORE research about this charm within ceremonial magick and Hoodoo traditions.

We've decided our intent, we've layed our compass and invited in the Witchfather and Witchmother, and other energies that we feel are going to help us. Now it's time to get to work. So, simply relax, stair at the sigil, the Abracadabra and let the image fade in and out. You will eventually see the image appear and then re-appear again, this is normal and natural. Your subconscious mind is soaking up the image and it's meaning, it's purpose and intent.

Now it's time to raise a little energy so we can direct it into our charm, with focused will and power. So depending on your intent of the spell/charm you can get as creative as you'd like with this. Come up with a chant/rhyme that is short, simple and in direct correlation with your intent. If you're not sure what to actually say, you can either chant

" It will be created in my words "

and visualize what it is that you are manifesting, bring to you, bringing down into your life. Once you feel you've raised enough energy, you've got the energy swirling around you, inside of your compass. Direct that energy straight into the charm/spell paper. Always, always make sure to visualize the END result, as if it's already yours because well, it IS already yours.

For me personally I created a charm I showed you all in my video. I had put a few herbs in there, a stone, a little bit of my own blood. I remember now that I did this manifesting spell/charm to see the beauty in life, the love and all the glory in this universe. I look back at it now and I see the results of this spell working PERFECTLY.

So that is it guy's and gal's! This is so simple, yet so powerful and effective. Get creative with this! Use whatever outline you are comfortable with. Use whichever deities you feel comfortable with. Remember to have fun with this. This is a group spell/experiment. If you have any further questions regarding this spell please don't hesitate to send me an email or message me on my public page.

Creating A Magickal Pouch

I Love Witchy Wednesdays and I hope you guys are too! It's been really amazing sharing all my stories and workings with you all! Here is a simple way to create a very powerful and effective Magickal Pouch!

1. Decide Your Intent

2. Never create a pouch for fun

3. Select the herbs that will help you and correspond to your working

4. Collect your herbs from the wild (or buy them)

5. Next infuse the herbs with intent and your energy.

Gather your herbs, and chant the following as you circle around your cauldron, counter clockwise, tossing your herbs in as you go...

" Round about the cauldron go,

in the herbs of magick throw,

Elfwort, trefoil, goatsleaf, bour,

in the pot the magick four

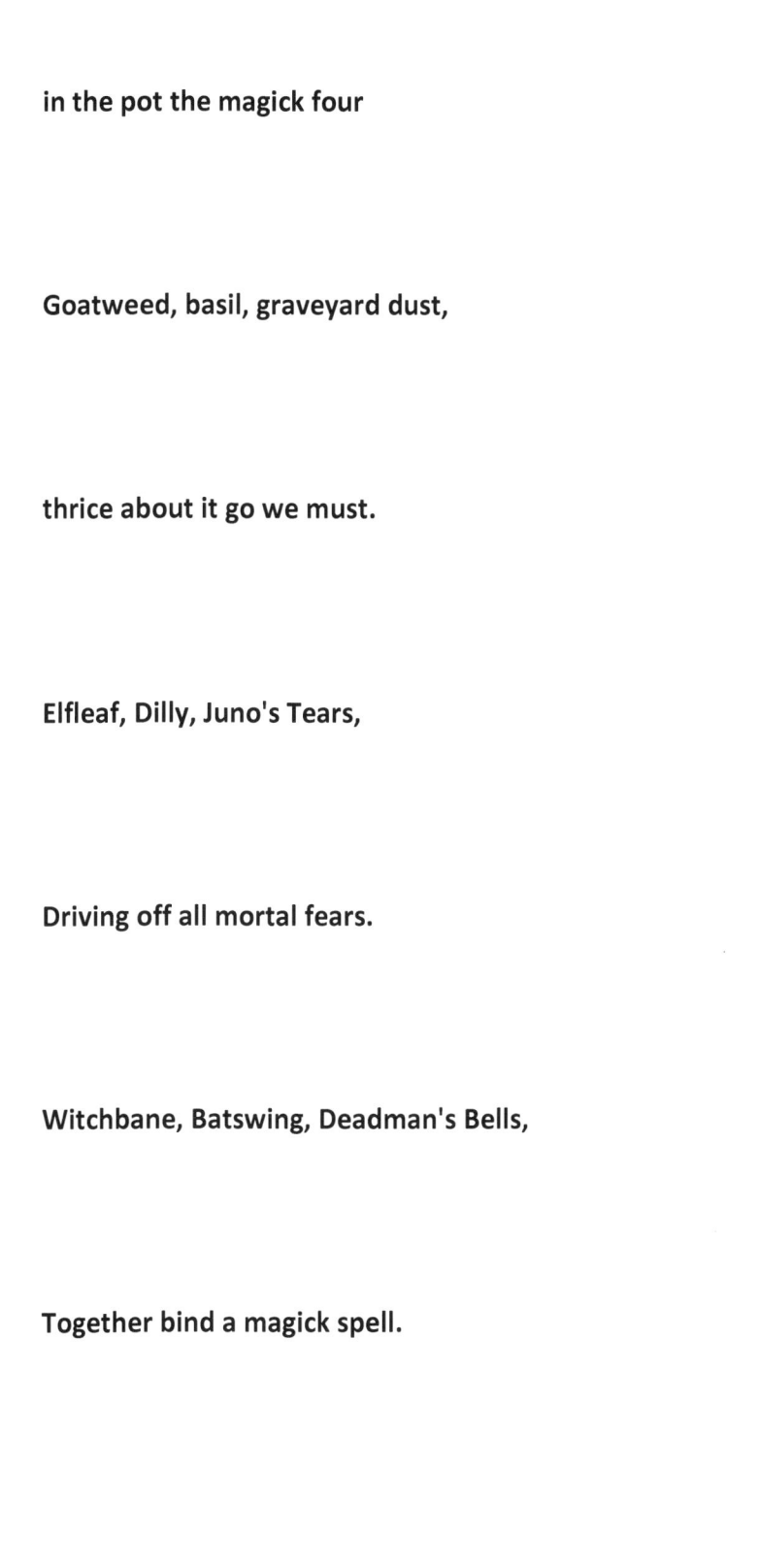

Goatweed, basil, graveyard dust,

thrice about it go we must.

Elfleaf, Dilly, Juno's Tears,

Driving off all mortal fears.

Witchbane, Batswing, Deadman's Bells,

Together bind a magick spell.

Thrice about the cauldron run,

Dance the dance and be it done! "

Scoop your mixture into a pouch, one you've created or one you've bought. You can carry this with you, hang it in your home, on your person, wherever you feel it should be.

The Witch's Foot and The Crossing

This shape is one of the most powerful symbols. the middle line running through the center is the God-Stane, stretching from Elfhame below to Chemeri above. This can be used to connect you with all the worlds and tremble the power around you. Realize the power connects you from your spine, to the powers above and below, power flows from all directions around you. The crossing is done thus;

1. Touch your forehead and name it the sky, the impregnator.

2. Touch your navel, and name it as the mother.

3. Touch your left shoulder and name it the puckerel

4. Touch your right shoulder and name it the other.

5. Fold your hands to your chest and call out to the wisdom and power of The Great Dark One.

6. Now with your breath take into yourself the spirit of the world, breathe it down into the place of your power, in your chest. Gather into yourself the power that endows, the whole world within motion, until it is a radiance from your chest. It will not feel as powerful as you'd like at first but keep doing it, gently. See this

giant ball of energy you have collected, form it ito the great Witch's Foot. See it inside your body, radiating out. A great way to feel power whenever you need to, knot and cord magick. All types of magick can be done using this very simple yet powerful technique.

Poppet Magick " The Little Spirit Doll "

The little soul or spirit doll you make to look exactly like yourself (or as close as possible), as well as if you are working on another individual. Once the doll is made it literally becomes you, or an extension of the person you've made it for. It needs to be treated like a child. Do not abandon it for a long period of time, nor leave it where people you don't trust can easily harm it. The clothes need to be kept clean and the environment as well. These dolls are made with parts of yourself (or said individual). Braid strands of hair into it's hair. Sew your finger nails into its fingers, etc. Boneset tea is the traditionl stuffing for these dolls.

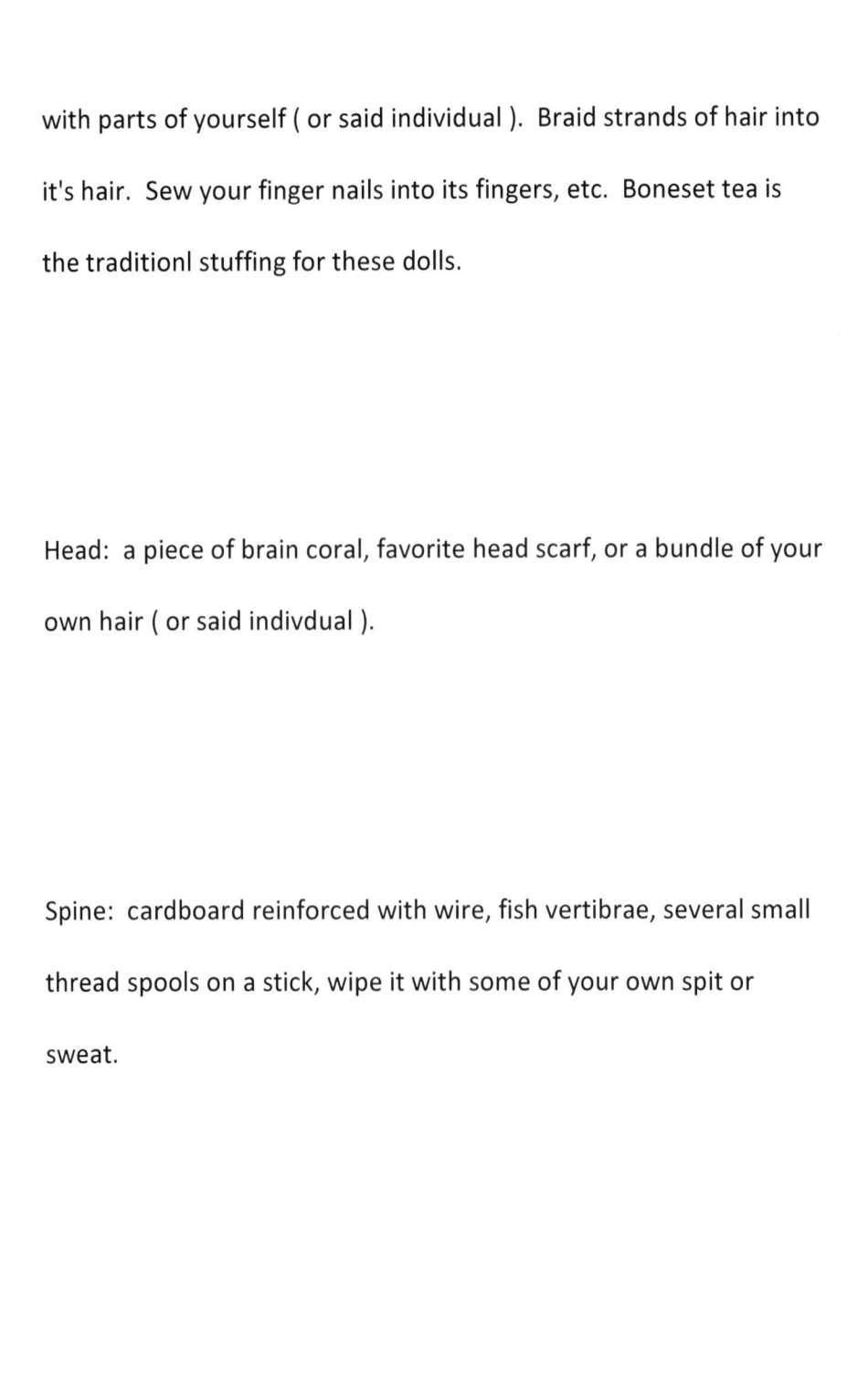

Head: a piece of brain coral, favorite head scarf, or a bundle of your own hair (or said indivdual).

Spine: cardboard reinforced with wire, fish vertibrae, several small thread spools on a stick, wipe it with some of your own spit or sweat.

Heart: A little red heart bag is made with dirt from your home, sugar, and blood pricked from your own finger, an Adam and Eve root, a piece of rose quartz.

Lungs: two pieces of sponge with your breath on them, two balloons with some seasame seeds in them.

Intestines: White yarn soaked in vegetable juice

Kindeys: Two pieces of clay mixed with your urine (or said individuals)

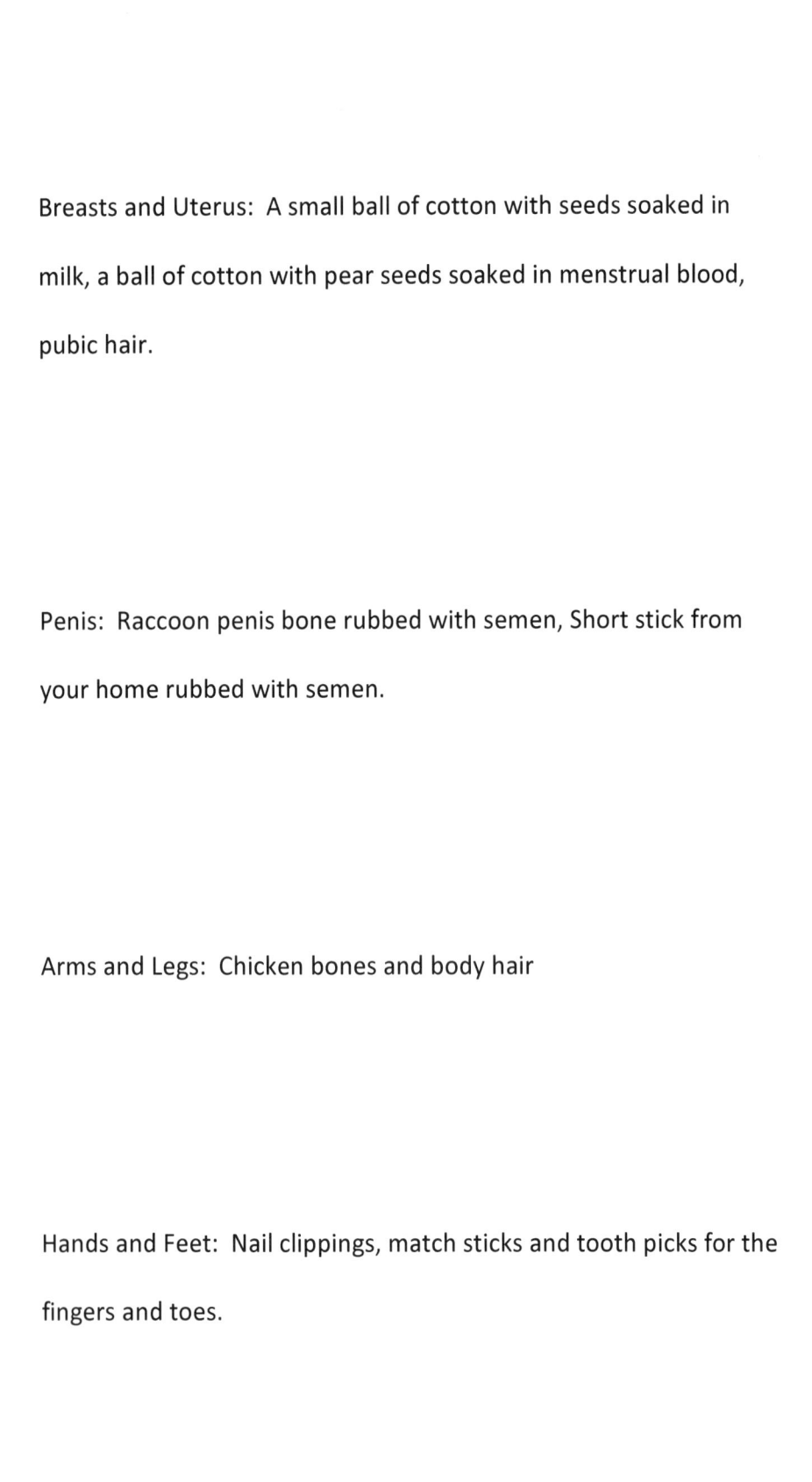

Breasts and Uterus: A small ball of cotton with seeds soaked in milk, a ball of cotton with pear seeds soaked in menstrual blood, pubic hair.

Penis: Raccoon penis bone rubbed with semen, Short stick from your home rubbed with semen.

Arms and Legs: Chicken bones and body hair

Hands and Feet: Nail clippings, match sticks and tooth picks for the fingers and toes.

Give the doll a secret name and cover it for 9 days. On the nineth day have a party for your doll. Invite close friends, ancestors, spirits and introduce the doll to them. Make your intention known to them.

Put the doll on you altar and feed him or her. Give it water and a candle. Have conversations with your doll. If you talk to your doll about problems you can expect two things; 1) Nobody will lie to you, 2) your business won't be dragged through the streets. Beyond that give your doll what you are asking for. If you want $100 give him/her 100 pennies and ask yur doll to multiply it. The same goes for healing, love, cleansing someone from a distance. Be creative with your doll and your process.

Spirit Encounter and Message

Spirit speaks to us in such strange ways. Sometimes we have no idea if it's our imagination or the actual spirit of the deceased. My little trick, in 20 years, I've learned to ask myself one questons " was this spirit? " . If my gut/heart says " yes " instantly I take that as a sure fire sign! Yes, Indeed this was from spirit.

A few nights ago I was on the verge of sleep and being awake. That state where you have no idea what is going on, all the colors, images, smells were so realistic, vivid, and so real! I used to work at

Sally's Beauty Supply and Equiptment, quite some years ago, about 5 years. We had an amazing boss, " Boss Lady " is what we called her. She really was such a great person. Even though her and I had our falling out, we did in fact make up and put everything in the past. Thank the gods for the last hug and the last " I love you ".

Make sure you tell your loved ones, pets, family members that you love them every-single-day of your life. You never know when someone's time is up here on this earth. Now, I know you are happy and warm again. So, here is what " Boss Lady " had to tell me. She came to me looking fabulous, as usual! Her hair white as snow, beautiful pink nails, as she would have had in this life. The whole time she's talking to me she's laughing and *cackling* like she used to. Very heart-warming to actually hear and smell her, and seeing her in the way she wanted to be seen.

I have no idea where we are, maybe in her house? Maybe in the store? My house? I don't think that's too awfully important but here is her message that she insisted got out.

" Ryan, honey, I am fine! Don't worry about me. I'm with my Mom, My Dad, My family. My time where you are is over, I won't be incarnating again. I am with God, The Lord. Please tell my family the more they hurt and grieve over me, I feel that pain. Tell them to please try, try for me to be happy. Go on living, don't let your lives (My Children) stop because my physical body is gone, that was just a vessel. I am so proud of my children for stepping up to the plate. They know I will always be with them. Make sure you let " Daloris " know how proud I am of her. The store is amazing, I couldn't have done it better. Big shoes to fill isn't it crazy ass white woman ? (She rolls her head back in laughter). Everyone needs to know I am fine and so will they be! I am not sad or upset that you didn't come to my funeral. You made the right choice. It was less pain for me to feel, radiating from you too. We do feel your sadness here. So, for me be happy, rembember me as I was when i was healthy. This is all I want. I want this message to get out. All my loved ones, children and employees (former), you are all so full of love. Keep on loving and living for me "

The whole time she's telling me the above message, she keeps rolling her head back in utter laughter, smiles and tons of hugs, just as she was when she was here on this earth. Well, " Boss Lady " your message is now out. You will always be loved and remembered in the best of light. We all love you so much! Rest in Power!

Using The Ouija Alone

Here lately I've noticed a lot of questions and comments popping up on using the Ouija alone. Is it ok to use this tool alone? Will you get " possessed ", will you open a " portal to hell " in your house? What about all the different paterns the Planchette glides about? Well, I am here to tell you a huge no. In my own mind, in the core of my being, a huge absloutely NOT.

First off I will tell you that you are going to need to check every-single fear you have, or might think you have, about the board, anything that you've heard and seen in the movies, please, disregard all of these " Ouijastitions ". Throw them all out the window. Hollywood has done enough damage to a perfectly safe tool, when used properly of course.

So, are all those fears gone yet? Didn't think so. One of the best ways that I've found to confront and face my own fears, about other subjects, not the Ouija, is Journaling. It sounds so simple you're thinking " well this isn't going to work ". If you write your fears out all on a sheet of paper, and ask yourself where do all these come from? Was I conditioned as a child to think this tool is evil? Did your religious background teach you it's an evil tool? Make sure you write all these things down, or even record yourself. I can almost guarentee you within a few months these " fears " will start to come up and surface. You will begin to know exactly why you are fearing certain things. This is about the best method I've found to work. Once you can acknowledge these fears, face them, then you can transmute them. You are turning your own demons into " Daemons ".

Ok, so we've faced our fears, checked how we're feeling the day we want to use the Board right? Fantastic! You never want to go into a session with anger, malice, hatred or fear. The board is only going to amplify these things from your subconcious, hence you being in more fear and panic than before. Plan out your session a day or two ahead. Make a rough outline of who you are going to speak with, stick with one specific entity to begin with. I really suggest an Angel (they will come to your aid if you just ask), your spirit guide, or a relative. Sticking with just ONE of these entities will be easier for you to validate the information you are recieving through the board.

So let's get over a few steps to ensure a safe and positive session, yeah? My biggest rule is ALWAYS go into a session knowing you are going to recieve only the best information, information that is going to serve you, better you and for your greatest good. If you don't have a sacred space or somewhere you can do this in a regular spot, on a regular basis, don't worry about it. Create that sacred space for yourself wherever you are, at anytime.

Personally I love lighting one candle in my tea-light, hymalayian Rock Salt holder. You can light as many candles as you want, put on some very soft, relaxing music, light your incense. Create that space that makes YOU feel; safe, positive and secure. Remember you are the one that is going to be attracting what you get through the board, not the other way around. You can have crucifixes around, rosaries, religious relics, anything you feel that will bring you protection. It is your intent that gives your items power.

So, we've prepared a sacred space where you will be contacting say your Spirit Guide. Start with any prayers you like, or you're comfortable with. Meditate, focus on your breath. Focus your energy into your breath and feel that going through your base chakra and up into your heart, let your heart open up, let it feel, breathe, see. Once you've put yourself into a slightly different altered state, go ahead and state your intentions. You could say something along the lines of this:

" I ask that only my Spirit Guide come through, only positive energies, for the greater good of all. "

You get the drift. Now you lightly place your fingers on the Planchette, call out, either in your heart or in words, to your ONE specific relative, Angel or Guide. Make sure to jot down any information you do get from the board. Video record yourself, or you can also use a tape recorder to record your session. The energy of the entity coming through is going to be VERY subtle. For some it may actually be pretty strong, others it may take years to even get the Planchette to move in just the slightest way. That's all OK! You have to remember that this tool requires paitence.

Don't second guess yourself, do not sit there thinking " it's just myself moving it ". Things like these are going to only set you back. If the Planchette starts to move in figure eight's, going through the numbers backwards, or even the alphabete, this is NOT NEGATIVE. Every-single entity has it's own " signature ". That is all that is, a spirit's signature, a thumb-print, just like your own.

Ok, so you've done your first Ouija Session by yourself and you got a bunch of gibberish. That's perfectly fine, again this is going to take time. You need this time to develope that trust with the one particular entity you are speaking with. Say you got a huge paragraph your first time (very unlikely but possible), research every-single thing you get through the board.

If you get anything that you might think is negative simply put the board away for that time. Say something like " thank you for your time and good bye ". It's as simple as that. Now, a lot of you will be saying " no you can't do this by yourself ", " no you are talking to demons, devils ". Wrong, you are not speaking with evil. Now if that is your intent you'll get what you ask for. Ending your session is pretty easy as well. Simply say something along the lines of "

Thank you for all that I've learned, thank you for coming, I wold like to say goodbye now ". The Planchette won't always go to " Goodbye". If you feel the need you can push it down to goodbye, afterall you want to feel safe and not afraid.

If you feel tired or drained after a session you can also eat someting afterwards, ground yourself back down to earth. You can blow out your candle, incense, clean up your space and prepare in advance for your next session. I really wanted to write this blog for those that cannot find someone whom they can trust to use the board with. I started using it by myself at 8 years old, I've never had a bad experience. I didn't have anyone to use the board with, so I really feel it's important for those out there that want to Ouija alone, to know my tips and how I prepare a session and close one.

Remember, I've been using this tool for 20 years. You are not going to recieve the fast pace movement of the Planchette quiet yet. Then again you just might! Take your time, research, read, get familiar with the Board itself, face down those fears and always be respectful to those that come and speak with you.

I wish you all the best of luck!

In Conclusion What is Ouija Pop?

A lot of people have been wondering what EXACTLY is Ouija Pop? Why the " Pop " after Ouija? Well! A very amazing fan of my YT channel asked and I responded. This is what my Holy Guardian Angel told me. Yes I have finally found out WHO my Holy Guardian Angel is! So strange too that it was just the other night as I wrote out the message....... So, again, What is OUIJA POP ? Here it goes.....

" Ouija Pop is my idea/concept of bringing the Ouija, Spirit Communications, Paganism, into a positive light through Modern Day Pop Culture... it's very inclusive.. Where people can be themselves and not feel judged or looked down on, instead we celebrate our differences. It is also an astral temple that has been built over a period of time, through this community. "

This is what Ouija Pop is. Ouija Pop is the art of bringing EVERYTHING that I practice, including using the board, tarot, Witchcraft, Paganism, Runes, Oils, into a better light through the usage of modern day Pop Culture. What better way to HONOR and RESPECT my " Youth " (my generation) and others as well, with a POSITIVE attitude and a healthy dose of respect for the Occult. NO the Occult is not " evil " or " negative ". Occult is Latin for " hidden

". So many get this confused and then become afraid and fearful of just about everything that the Occult compasses. I like to think of the word Occult as being an umbrella for so many things that we do and do not understand.

All genders, religions, races, creeds, ethnic backgrounds are welcome. It is a place for YOU to come and feel FREE. Free to celebrate OUR differences in one another. I think I've accomplished this quite well through " Ouija Pop ". There WILL be a short film (it is currently in the works), about Ouija Pop as well! Are YOU interested in being a part of the movement? If so let your freak flag FLY HIGH!!! Be proud of YOURSELF. You are amazing, beautiful, unique, and respected here FOR all of your flaws and all.

I Love You Ouija Poppers!!!

Printed in Great Britain
by Amazon